ISBN 978-1-330-73637-1
PIBN 10098733

Forgotten Books is a registered trademark of FB &c Ltd.
Copyright © 2018 FB &c Ltd.
FB &c Ltd, Dalton House, 60 Windsor Avenue, London, SW19 2RR.
Company number 08720141. Registered in England and Wales.

For support please visit www.forgottenbooks.com

1 MONTH OF
FREE
READING

at

www.ForgottenBooks.com

By purchasing this book you are eligible for one month membership to ForgottenBooks.com, giving you unlimited access to our entire collection of over 1,000,000 titles via our web site and mobile apps.

To claim your free month visit:

www.forgottenbooks.com/free98733

THE

WAR IN EUROPE:

BEING A

RETROSPECT OF WARS AND TREATIES,

SHOWING THE

REMOTE AND RECENT CAUSES AND OBJECTS

OF A

DYNASTIC WAR,

IN CONNECTION WITH

THE BALANCE OF POWER IN EUROPE.

BY A. J. H. DUGANNE.

NEW YORK:

ROBERT M. DE WITT, 160 & 162 NASSAU STREET.

1859.

CONTENTS.

W. H. TINSON, Printer and Stereotyper, 43 & 45 Centre Street.

EUROPE IN THE PRESENT CENTURY.

I.

THE aspect of European affairs at the present time is of moral and material significance to all the world. In a progressive age like this in which we live, when mind and matter quiver under daily impulses of knowledge and science, all civilization must be affected, more or less, by a struggle for empire between two hostile powers like France and Austria. Many questions and consequences are involved in the conflict of dynasties—various speculations are ventured concerning results to ensue—and numberless hopes and fears hang trembling on the poise of expectation, both in Europe and our own land. The war now devastating Italy may be regarded as a game of tremendous hazard, whereon the Old and New World have stakes of vast consequence to their future weal or woe.

II.

If a feeling of national interest is shared by American as well as foreign states, it is, likewise, equally felt by our adopted and native citizens. German, French, Italian and other continental people, who constitute so large a portion of our communities, have indeed the force of former associations and ties of kindred to connect them personally with actors and localities of the contest ; but American-born patriots are not behind in recognizing the crisis to be one peculiarly worthy of their consideration as members of a democratic confederation.

III.

It lacks just a lustrum of half a century since the Peace of Europe was said to be definitively settled by the treaties entered into between the allied conquerors of Napoleon Bonaparte. Dictating terms to France in her own capital, the four victorious powers—Russia, England, Prussia, and Austria—deprived their former rival of all acquisitions she had made since the revolution of 1792, exiled her emperor to Elba, and restored Bourbon rule in the person of Louis XVIII. On the 3d of March, 1814, the allies took possession of Paris ; on the 2d of October, they met by their representatives, in the Congress of Vienna, and in March, 1815, their deliberations were suddenly interrupted by the intelligence that Bonaparte had broken the treaty, by leaving Elba, and was advancing with an army through France to regain his lost power.

IV.

Louis XVIII. fled from his capital to Flanders ; Napoleon signed the new French Constitution, and submitted his right to the throne to popular vote. He was sustained by a million and a half affirmative votes against less than half a million negative.   On the 1st of June, 1815, he found himself at the head of 560,000 men, and at once led 217,000 against the allied armies of England, Prussia, and Russia.   A million effective soldiers, including a Prussian army, of 100,000, under Blucher and about an equal force of British, Germans, and Belgians under Wellington, were advancing to unite on the French frontier. Bonaparte marched against Blucher with 120,000 men, and defeated him at Ligny, June 16th.   On the eighteenth he encountered Wellington and Blucher combined, and lost the battle of Waterloo.

V.

The die was cast against him.   He fled to Paris, abdicated in favor of his son, and was shortly after captured at sea by the British, and exiled to St. Helena. Louis XVIII. went back to his throne, and the Congress of Vienna resumed its deliberations.   The three powers of Central Europe, Austria, Prussia, and Russia, entered into a treaty of alliance, September 26, 1815, by which they bound themselves for mutual assistance in case of any attempt at revolution on the part of their subjects.   The treaty was approved though not subscribed by England.   Before noticing the basis of Peace Settlement made by the Congress of Vienna, I shall glance at the position of various nations affected by the treaties of 1815, leaving France, as we have seen, reduced to her territorial limits as they existed before the revolution, her Bourbons being restored, and the line of Bonaparte declared incapable of reigning.

VI.

Great Britain, anterior to the battle of Waterloo, was chief head of the anti-Napoleon league, her cabinet dictating campaigns, her armies in the van of action, her purse relied on by bankrupt confederates.   She had disputed the progress of French empire for more than twenty years, maintaining often single-handed, an uncompromising war against Bonaparte's ambition.   By supporting, almost unaided, the enormous expenses of campaigns in Syria and the Spanish Peninsula, maintaining fleets in all seas, and armies in several countries—she had increased her National Debt from £200,000,000 to nearly £900,000,000 ; beside swelling her annual tax budget from £17,000,000 to £77,000,000 ; her aggregate of disbursements throughout the war amounting to the enormous sum of £17,000,000,000 sterling.   Such colossal sacrifices of treasure, without computation of losses in human life and by burdens entailed upon an impoverished population at home, were England's contribution to the League of Sovereigns.   Her reward was the meretricious glory of Waterloo— a victory which, though it promised " security for the future," was surely no adequate " indemnity for the past."   The fifteen hundred million francs exacted from Louis XVIII., for his restored kingdom, was scarcely a *quid pro quo* for all that Great Britain had expended ; for she had been the master spirit of a coalition which successively arrayed with herself against Napoleon, the governments of Russia, Austria, Sweden, Prussia, Spain, Portugal, Naples, and a German League of minor Powers ; she had inspired and strengthened them all, till her crowning victory overthrew the common adversary forever.   Yet, hardly were the echoes of Waterloo silent than she found herself confronted by the jealousy of continental states that owed their very existence to her fidelity and fortitude. Austrian diplomacy over-matched Great Britain's influence in the Congress of Vienna, denying in council what she had earned on the field—the position of chief adviser, if not arbiter in continental reconstruction. The great commissary and paymaster of the war remained, at the peace, only its principal bankrupt.

VII.

Noticing the various nations whose interests are more or less involved in the turmoil or quiet of Europe, we may arrive at a definite idea as to their positions in a general conflict. It will be recollected that the territorial limits of each of the continental powers, as well as its weight in the European balance, were fixed by the treaties of 1815, and that the parties to the great settlement bound themselves by solemn oaths not only to preserve inviolate each condition of their mutual pact, as individual governments, but, moreover, to unite their power at any future time, to prevent the least infringement of that pact. By this means the Congress of Vienna, in 1814–15, organized what became afterward known as the Balance of Power in Europe ; and the three principal continental powers subscribed a treaty of confederation on which was bestowed the name of Holy Alliance. We shall leave the settlement and its treaties for another connection, in order to glance at the dynasties of Continental Europe.

VIII.

The present RUSSIAN DYNASTY is that of Holstein-Gotthorp. Russian or Muscovite sovereignty was founded by Ruric, a barbarian prince, during the ninth century. Wladimir the Great, called the Russian Solomon, reigned in the eleventh century, and was converted to Christianity through the Greek Church, which afterward became the religion of his subjects. Russian rulers were called Dukes of Muscovy till the reign of Ivan IV., who took the title of CZAR, which signifies nothing less than CÆSAR. It was assumed by Ivan in token of his claims to the Eastern Roman Empire, bequeathed to his father by Alexis, a fugitive scion of the Emperors of Constantinople, deposed by the Turks. Since the time of Ivan, Russian ambition has never lost sight of Constantinople as a future seat of Asiatic empire. After Ivan came the House of Romanoff, of which Peter the Great was second monarch, and his daughter, Elizabeth, last. Peter III., son of Peter the Great's daughter Anne and her husband, a Duke of Holstein-Gotthorp, then founded the present dynasty ; but soon lost crown and life, leaving Catherine II. empress in 1762. Catherine made war against Turkey, partitioned Poland, and left her throne to Paul I., who joined the coalition against republican France, and afterward made peace with her. He was murdered by conspirators in 1801, and his son, Alexander I., succeeded to a throne threatened by the armies of Napoleon Bonaparte. Alexander entered into alliance with Napoleon in 1807, at the Treaty of Tilsit, but abandoned him in 1812, and provoked the campaign of Moscow. After Bonaparte's retreat from Moscow, the Russian emperor pursued him, and entered Paris with the Allies in 1814. Alexander I. died in 1825, and Nicholas I. became Czar, and reigned till the late war between Russia and the allied powers of England, France, and Turkey. Nicholas pushed Russian pretensions farther toward Constantinople, and crushed out the nationality of Poland. He left the empire to his son, Alexander II., present Czar. The Russian Empire covers an area of 8,000,000 square miles, of which nearly two-thirds are in Asia, with 60,000,000 inhabitants.

IX.

The family of HAPSBURG, the reigning DYNASTY OF AUSTRIA, was originally headed by a simple count of the German Empire. The German emperors were formerly elected by votes of the princes, dukes, counts, and marquises of the country, convened for the purpose. In 1273, Count Rodolph of Hapsburg was chosen Emperor of Germany. Since that time the family has aggrandized itself greatly through marriage, and reduced large territories under its sway through war or diplomacy.. Albert I. of Austria tyrannized over Switzerland, but lost that country in the fourteenth century through a general revolt of the cantons. Charles V., his descendant, was likewise King of Spain. Ferdinand I., his successor, united Bohemia and Hungary with Austria proper. The ambitious projects of Austria brought on the celebrated Thirty Years' War—between 1618 and 1648. Under Charles VI., a century later, Austria and Spain were again united. He left the throne of Austria to his daughter, Maria Theresa. She married Francis of Lorraine, Grand Duke of Tuscany. The House of Austro-Lorraine now occupies the throne, represented by Francis Joseph. The possessions of Austria consist of a number of states, foreign to each other, whose independence has been destroyed at various times by the craft or violence of the House of Hapsburg. Among others which make up the bulk of empire, are Upper and Lower Austria, Bohemia, the mountain provinces of Styria, Carynthia, and the Tyrol, the ancient kingdom of Hungary, a half-dozen southern provinces extending to the frontier of Turkey, a third part of old Poland, under the name of Gallicia, and, finally, the Austro-Italian or Lombardo-Venetian Kingdom. The scattered and diverse populations amount to about thirty-five millions of souls, in a geographical area of about 256,339 square miles. The map of Europe will show Austria's position. It lies between Russia on the northeast, and Turkey on the south, with Prussia and the other German States northwest. Austria is accessible from Russia along its whole Polish and Gallician border. It is entered from France through Savoy, Sardinia, or the Rhenish States.

X.

Leaving the Danube above Vienna, we come to the GERMAN STATES, including Prussia, Saxony, and the Free Cities. The German Confederation, so called, recognizes Austria as its chief, but the real German portion of Austrian population or territory is comparatively small. In fact, Austria claims position as head of the Germanic Confederation more by force of military prestige than because of affinity between the bulk of its inhabitants and those of Germany proper. The Confederation of 1815 grew out of a league against Bonaparte, made in 1806, by all the potentates of Middle Germany. The Confederation comprises thirty-four monarchical states, and the Free Cities. They compose a Congress, to which each power sends delegates, who cast votes in the ratio of the political importance of the state which they represent. The Confederation was organized for mutual safety of the German States in time of war.

XI.

Coöperating in the league against France, Frederick William III. of Prussia represented in 1815 the DYNASTY OF BRANDENBURG-HOHENZOLLERN. Prussia had then been governed by kings just one century, having been originally a dukedom, tributary to the monarchs of Poland. Frederick William, defeated at Jena, subsequently ceded a part of his realm to France at the Treaty of Tilsit. After the return of Bonaparte from Moscow, the Prussian monarch, assisted by a patriotic army of the German nation, organized in the "Tugend-Bund," or "League of Virtue," joined the grand combination against France. Frederick William III. reigned till 1840, and was succeeded by Frederick William IV. Prussia comprises East and West Prussia, Posen, Pomerania, Brandenburg, Silesia, Westphalia, and several districts on the Rhine, together with the portion of Poland which fell to her share at the tripartite dismemberment of that kingdom. The aggregate extent of Prussian territory is 106,852 square miles; but most of this is sparsely populated, with exposed frontiers, liable to sudden attack from either Russia, Austria, or France.

XII.

The three States of SWEDEN, NORWAY, and DENMARK, occupy a frontier, as regards Russia, which may directly involve them in any general struggle. Norway lies parallel with Sweden, both countries covering a peninsula, washed on the west and north by the North Sea and Atlantic, and on the east by the Baltic and Gulf of Bothnia. They are thus opposite the west seacoast of Russia. Denmark, further south, is situated on the peninsula of Jutland, which protrudes from the Netherlands and Upper Germany into the mouth of the Baltic. It is of importance to Russia and France in alliance, to secure the coöperation of the three northern kingdoms, and likewise that of Holland and Belgium, which border on French territory. If Denmark espouse the French side, as in 1801, the Netherlandish provinces are menaced at once. If Norway and Sweden be controlled by Russia, the North Sea will open to Alexander's fleets, and the Prussian frontier, Hanover, and other German states, would lie exposed to every attack. In this way Austria and Germany would be hemmed in on every side by hostile powers. A consultation of the map of Europe will show that Central Germany could thus be made the battle-ground of continental dynasties.

XIII.

DENMARK is probably the oldest kingdom in Europe preserving ancient limits. Its people were warlike in ancient times of their history, and swarmed out as invaders of the British Isles and France. They embraced Christianity during the tenth century. A Danish king named Sweyn conquered England, and his son Canute added Norway to his dominions, wielding three sceptres at the same time. England afterward became independent; but in the fourteenth century, Denmark, Norway, and Sweden were united under one sovereign; afterward Sweden was detached, and the German provinces of Schleswig-Holstein gained. At the beginning of the present century, the King of Denmark refused to enter into the coalition of northern powers against Bonaparte. To intimidate him, England sent out a squadron under Nelson, which bombarded Copenhagen and seized the Danish fleet. But the Danes still adhered to the French side, and in 1814 the Allied Powers punished their contumacy, by taking away Norway, to bestow upon Bernadotte, the King of Sweden. The German duchy of Lauenburg was given to Denmark, as an indemnity for the spoliation. Norway and Sweden now constitute one kingdom, under the rule of Oscar I., son of Charles John, who was formerly one of Bonaparte's marshals. Sweden's history, under various monarchs, is united now with that of Norway. The united kingdom measures 1,550 miles in length, by about 350 in breadth. Denmark and the duchies Schleswig-Holstein and Lauenburg comprise about 17,375 square miles.

XIV.

We now comprehend the localities of NORTHERN EUROPE, down to the Netherlands, which divide them from France. It will be understood that one large Russian army is concentrated upon the Gallician or Austrian frontier, and another on the Vistula, near the Silesian or Prussian frontier. Along the whole German frontier, a line of Russian military stations, half a mile apart, is established. Sentinels continually pace from one station to another, and patrols of cavalry traverse the entire border. These preparations seem to menace all Germany. A Russian fleet in the Baltic might coöperate with its land forces for a like purpose ; while a Russian force in the Black Sea threatens the Danubian Principalities. On the French side, the "Army of Italy" invests Austria in her Lombardo-Venetian kingdom ; while another French army could be thrown through Belgium and over the Rhine into the heart of Germany.

XV.

Holland and Belgium formed a Gallic province under Imperial Rome, and afterward became a portion of Charlemagne's Frankish dominions. Subsequently they were broken into several small sovereignties ; there being a king of Friesland, a Duke of Brabant, a Count of Flanders, a Count of Holland, warring against one another, till Philip, King of France, united them with his territories, under the name of Low Countries. Flanders afterward passed to Austria by marriage, Spain claimed Holland for a like reason, and the result was a civil war, ending in the establishment of a republic by the Holland States, under a chief called the Stadtholder, by the Treaty of Westphalia or Munster, in 1648. The republic flourished, and founded colonies in America, settling, among others, the territory now occupied by New York, New Jersey, Rhode Island, Pennsylvania, and Delaware. Stadtholder William III. ended the republic, by establishing hereditary succession to the Stadtholdership. This prince subsequently resigned the crown of Holland to his son, and took possession of the English throne, after expulsion of his father-in-law, James II., last of the Stuart Dynasty. In 1795, a French revolutionary army, under General Pichegru, assisted the people of Holland in erecting the Batavian Republic, so called. In 1806, Napoleon I. organized the seven provinces into a kingdom for his brother, Louis Bonaparte, and three years afterward deposed him, incorporating the Belgian monarchy with the French Empire. In 1814, the Congress of Vienna reërected the Low Countries, or Netherlands, into a kingdom, and bestowed the sovereignty on William I. In 1830, Belgium revolted, and formed an independent kingdom under Leopold of Saxe-Coburg. Holland and Belgium have since remained separate. Holland is that portion of territory which lies northeast of the Rhine ; Belgium, southwest, and close to France. The entire extent of both countries is 24,870 square miles. The people of Belgium speak French generally. Holland claims the two German provinces of Luxemburg and Limburg, dividing it from Rhenish German States.

XVI.

Leaving France on the southwest, we cross the Pyrenees, and enter upon that southern extremity of the European continent, which is formed by the

Spanish Peninsula. Traversing Spain westwardly to the river Tagus, beyond Madrid, we reach Portugal, which lies on the Atlantic. The Spanish Peninsula has the Straits of Gibraltar and the Mediterranean on its south and east, while the Atlantic and Bay of Biscay wash its western and northern shores. If France should extend her dynastic rule beyond the Pyrenees, as under Napoleon I., she would possess uninterrupted dominion of the European Continent, from Belgium to the Mediterranean, and across that sea to her African territory of Algeria. Add the Italian Peninsula to this, and France would control the entire seaboard of Continental Europe, from the British Channel to the Grecian Archipelago. Russian maritime conquest might here begin, and extend through the Dardanelles to the Black Sea. Russian maritime control might likewise continue that of France north of the British Channel, through the Danish Sound to the Baltic. In this manner, the allied dynasties of France and Russia might absolutely lay claim to the naval sceptre of Europe, Africa, and Asia, confining Great Britain to her Islands, and compressing Germany by an ever-narrowing cordon of hostile encroachments. Such was the policy which Napoleon I. sought to carry into operation, but failed because of Russia's withdrawal from alliance with France. Such a policy, at this time, is foreshadowed by the remarkable understanding that seems to exist between Alexander II. and Napoleon III. If it be developed by coöperative military operations on the part of the two emperors, it must compel the continental powers to take sides. In this event, Norway and Sweden would probably be brought under Russian influence ; Denmark, Belgium, and perhaps Holland, be controlled by France ; whilst revolutionary action would be encouraged throughout the Spanish and Italian peninsulas. Austria and Germany must then await the discretion of the allies, or call upon Great Britain to protract the struggle by lending her assistance, as in the war against Napoleon I.

XVII.

SPAIN, settled originally by Phœnicians, Carthagenians, and Romans, was afterward overrun by Germanic barbarians, Visigoths and Saracens. The Moors were expelled about the same time that America was discovered, and Spain became a leading power in Europe. The family of Hapsburg, or Austria, succeeded to the Spanish throne, by marriage, in 1564, and an Austrian dynasty ruled till 1700, when Philip V., a Bourbon prince, ascended the throne. The Bourbons held sovereignty till ousted by Napoleon I., who made his brother Joseph King of Spain in 1808. In 1814, the Allied Powers reëstablished Ferdinand VII., the exiled Bourbon monarch. Isabella succeeded Ferdinand. Civil war has since raged throughout the kingdom, at intervals, but a liberal constitution has been gained by the people.

XVIII.

PORTUGAL, like other countries of Southern Europe, was overrun successively by ancient Germans and Goths, and later by Moors from Africa. In the eleventh century an independent Christian kingdom was established, and has since continued under three dynasties. The last was that of Braganza, expelled by a French army under General Massena, and obliged to take refuge in the Portuguese vice-royalty of Brazil ; but restored to the throne after Bonaparte's overthrow. A civil war of succession took place at a later date ; Don Miguel usurped the throne in 1828, and was succeeded by Doña Maria in 1832.

XIX.

Crossing the Alps from France into Italy, we enter through Savoy into Sardinia and Piedmont. This district was anciently so flourishing and fertile that it was called " the nursery of Rome," " the mother of flocks," and " the favorite of Ceres." At the decline of the Roman Empire, the province passed successively under dominion of Vandals, Goths and Moors. It was afterward contended for by the rival Italian cities of Genoa and Pisa, and in the 13th century, Pope Boniface VIII. bestowed its sovereignty on Don Pedro IV., King of Arragon. Pedro allowed it a representative government, and it flourished as much as it was possible under feudal usages. When Arragon became united with other Spanish provinces, under a single monarch, Sardinia remained tributary, governed by viceroys, till the 18th century. In 1720, it passed under sway of Victor Amadeus II., King of Sicily and Savoy. Under Charles Emanuel, Victor's son, the kingdom comprised Sardinia, Savoy, Piedmont, Montserrat, and several smaller districts ; but after the battle of Marengo, Bonaparte confined the king, Victor Emanuel V., to the *island* of Sardinia, and annexed his continental territory of Piedmont to France. By the treaties of 1815, Victor Emanuel regained sovereignty over Piedmont and Savoy, but was obliged to abdicate in favor of his brother, Charles Felix, in 1821. Charles Albert placed himself at the head of a liberal movement in 1848–9. The Sardinian States under Italian dominion comprise Piedmont, Genoa, Savoy, and the island of Sardinia. The capital city is Turin—Victor Emanuel VI. is king. Genoa, the present naval rendezvous of the French in Italy, occupies the southeastern seaboard of Sardinia. The Republic of Genoa long disputed with Venice the sovereignty of middle-age commerce. It maintained its independence till 1740, when it was subdued by Austria, after having given up the island of Corsica to France. Napoleon erected it into a commonwealth, under name of Ligurian Republic, and afterward annexed it to France. In 1815 it was given, together with Piedmont, to Victor Emanuel V., by the allies, and has since shared the fortunes of Sardinia.

XX.

Passing through Upper Sardinia, or Savoy, we enter upon the Swiss Federal Republic, known in ancient times as Helvetia. The Franks, who founded the French monarchy, also subdued Switzerland, but the territory was subsequently annexed to the German Empire. During the fourteenth century, Albert, Count of Hapsburg, a German noble, usurped dominion over all the German cantons, but his tyranny was overthrown by a revolt under William Tell. The Swiss cantons afterward formed a league, and have since resisted all attempts of French or German princes to deprive them of their liberties. At present the Swiss Confederation comprises twenty-two cantons, or provinces, each sovereign and independent within its own borders, but leagued in a commonwealth of mutual defence. The house of Austria acknowledged the nationality of Switzerland at the peace of Westphalia, in 1648. In 1799, Napoleon I. invaded the Republic with his army, and imposed a new constitution upon the cantons. The limits, rights, and duties of the Swiss Confederation were finally settled by the congress of allied powers, at Vienna, in 1815.

XXI.

Descending from Tyrolese Switzerland into Italy, we find ourselves in the Lombardo-Venetian kingdom, under Austrian domination. This territory is subdivided into the governments of Milan, Venice, Parma, and Modena. It extends south as far as the Papal States and Tuscany. Its capital, MILAN, was a powerful province as far back as Roman times. During the middle ages it became a republic, and resisted successive German invasions, under Frederick Barbarossa, and other emperors. It was subsequently controlled by a line of dukes, till 1714, when it passed under Austrian domination. In 1797, Milan was made the centre of a Cisalpine Republic, established by French arms, and in 1804 became the capital of a new kingdom of Italy, intended by Napoleon I. as an appanage for his son. In 1814 Milan was restored to Austria by the Congress of Vienna, and became the chief city of Austrian Lombardy. . . . The VENETIAN REPUBLIC of medieval times, fell into decay long before the beginning of this century, but the French abolished the doge-ship in 1797. By the treaty of Campo-Formio, in that year, General Bonaparte ceded Venice to Austria, but by that of Presbourg, at a later date, it was returned to the French emperor, who bestowed it on his step-son, Eugene de Beauharnais. In 1814–15 the Congress of Vienna reëstablished it as second city of the Lombardo-Venetian kingdom, under Austria.

XXII.

The states of Tuscany, Modena, Parma, and Lucca, were left by the treaties of 1815 as nominally independent principalities, but have since been brought, more or less directly, under Austrian control. TUSCANY was an ancient Roman province, and passed afterwards under Goths and Lombards, till Charlemagne made it a marquisate or border district, of his Frankish empire. Subsequently Roman popes and German emperors laid claim to its ownership. Their struggles for possession gave rise to the two great Italian parties, called Guelfs and Ghibelines, whose quarrels involved all Italy in civil strife. During the 12th century the Tuscan people established a free state, known as the Florentine Republic, but a succession of the Medici family afterward ruled the country as dukes, till the last prince of that house bequeathed his sovereignty to Austria. Tuscany was overrun by a French army, under the Directory, and in 1801 was erected into the Etrurian kingdom, for Louis Duke of Parma. It was afterward annexed to France by Napoleon I., and in 1814 was made an Austrian grand duchy by the Congress of Vienna. . . . . . PARMA was a republic in the 12th century, and was active in the civil wars between Guelfs and Ghibelines. The Popes claimed it as their territory, but Paul III. was satisfied to behold his son made its duke. A succession of dukes governed the state till it fell, with Lucca, into French hands. After Napoleon's fall, the Congress of Vienna gave Parma to Maria Louisa, ex-Empress of France, who belonged to the Austrian royal family. When she died, in 1847, it passed to the present claimants of the throne. . . . . . LUCCA was left by the Congress of Vienna as a small independent principality, to revert under certain conditions to Tuscany, of which it now forms a portion. . . . . Ravenna, Ferrara, and other papal states on the Tuscan and Lombard border, are mainly under influence of Austria. All these central Italian states have jealous local restrictions of trade and intercourse. Between the French Alps and Florence, capital of Tuscany, a traveller is subject to custom-house regulations of Piedmont, Lombardy, Parma, Modena, and Tuscany. To get from Leghorn in Tuscany, up to Genoa, he must pass through five different states in a distance of 150 miles.

XXIII.

Leaving Austrian Italy, we enter the States of the Church, under sovereignty of the Pope of Rome. The chief cities are Bologna, Ancona, Ravenna, Perugia, Ferrara, and some smaller towns. The boundaries of the Papal States have changed at various periods, under different Popes, but in 1815 were fixed by the Congress of Vienna. They have since been under Austrian influence, to a greater or less extent, as circumstances have favored German pretensions over the whole of Italy. Pope Pius IX. distinguished the opening of his reign, by inaugurating many political reforms ; but he became subsequently influenced by a reactionary spirit which followed the Revolution of 1848. The Roman States were declared a republic in 1848, under a Triumvirate, consisting of Mazzini, Avezzana, and Garibaldi. The interference of Austria and France overturned the government, and Pope Pius was restored to his throne by a French army under General Oudinot. The Triumvirate were dispersed. Mazzini took refuge in England where he has since remained. Avezzana returned to the United States, his previous residence. Garibaldi also visited the United States, but afterwards sailed to Genoa, his native state, as captain of a merchant ship. He now commands a division of the Sardinian Army. Pius IX. remains still in the Papal Chair at Rome, guarded by French troops since his restoration.

XXIV.

South and east of the Roman States we enter the kingdom of NAPLES. Its territory formed part of the earlier conquests of ancient Rome. After the decline of that empire, it passed successively under the yoke of Lombard barbarians, and Saracens. In the eleventh century, two Norman knights, with their followers, drove out the infidels, and established a Christian kingdom, dividing the sovereignty. This was the origin of the Neapolitan monarchy. The Island of SICILY, originally settled by Greeks, became subsequently a battle-ground between Carthaginians and Romans. Barbarian and Saracen invasions followed, until Normans won the country as they had won Naples. Sicily and Naples were then united under one sovereignty, forming the KINGDOM OF THE TWO SICILIES. The crown passed through a succession of French, German, and Spanish families, until Charles V., Emperor of Germany and Spain, bequeathed it to his Austrian successors. Austrian dynasties alternated with Bourbons till 1806, when Joseph Bonaparte, first, and Joachim Murat, next, were placed on the throne by Napoleon I. Ferdinand, the deposed monarch, was restored by the Congress of Vienna. He died in 1820, and was succeeded by his grandson, the present tyrant, who has grievously oppressed the country.

XXV.

Take the map of Europe, and observe the position, as regards each other, of the various dominions that are here briefly noticed. More than one half the geographical area is occupied by Russia's gigantic territory, west of the Ural Mountains. At the southern extremity of Russia is the CRIMEA, theatre of the last Turkish war. The ambition of the Czars has always aimed at encroachment upon Turkish principalities bordered by the Black Sea and by the Austrian frontier. Russia coveted a passage to Constantinople through the rich vale of the Danube. Turkey and the Grecian peninsula would thus be comprised in her empire, and the Adriatic and Mediterranean opened to Russian fleets. To gain these advantages of sea-coast, would be to command both Europe and Asia from the Caspian Sea to the Mediterranean.

XXVI.

Tracing Russia's borders from Odessa on the Black Sea, along the line of the Danube, we cross the Danubian Principalities ; these join the military frontier of Austria, and form the northern circuit of Turkish possessions in Europe. Austrian territory extends northward to Silesia and westward to the German States and Swiss Republic. It includes the military frontier, Croatia, Hungary, Transylvania, Bohemia, Wallachia, Gallicia, and, northward, part of divided Poland. The districts surrounding Vienna contain a German population ; those east of the Danube comprise Sclavic and other races, more or less alien from central communities.

XXVII.

Austria commands the Gulf of Venice, by her sea-port and naval depot of Trieste. Military supplies can be shipped from that port, and recruits from the port of Fiume, in the gulf of that name. Austrian borders join that portion of the Italian Peninsula known as the Lombardo-Venetian Kingdom, or Austrian Italy. This comprises all the Adriatic coast to the river Po. South of the Po, the Adriatic bounds the Papal States down to the confines of Naples. Austrian Italy extends inland in a westerly direction, till it reaches Sardinia, separated from it by the river Ticino. It penetrates the peninsula west of the Papal States, till it strikes the Grand Duchy of Tuscany. West of the Ticino, Sardinian territory extends through Savoy to the borders of France ; southwardly from the Swiss Alps, it goes down through Piedmont and Genoa to the Mediterranean Sea. Sardinia also owns an island of that name, lying south of Corsica, in the Tuscan Sea.

XXVIII.

The river Ticino lies between the famous battle-fields of Lodi and Marengo. Following the Bormida River, southwesterly from Marengo, we reach the first three battle-fields of the great Napoleon—Mondovi, Milessimo, and Montenotte. Going west from this locality, we trace the route that Bonaparte pursued from the French Alps to MILAN. We recognize the opening of the present war as similar to that of 1796. In one month of that year the young republican general gained his three battles. Bonaparte ended the Italian war by forcing Austria, after the Battle of Arcola, to submit to a humiliating peace. Venice and Lombardy were evacuated by the Austrians, and an Italian democracy was established, under the name of Cisalpine Republic. In the present war, the French and Sardinian armies awaited Austrian invasion from Lombardy. The act of invasion consisted in the passage of the Ticino. The French-Sardinian forces remained intrenched between Turin and the Po. The seat of war is narrow, and contains the principal battle-fields whereon Napoleon I. achieved his first victories.

XXIX.

The theatre of war, thus disclosed, occupies a space less than thirty miles square. The whole of Sardinia is not more than one hundred miles from east to west borders—that is, from the river Ticino, which divides it from Austrian territory, to the French frontier. It is but little more than that distance from the upper or Swiss frontier to the seaboard of Genoa. At the commencement of hostilities, the French army was posted west of Briancon, near the French border, and the main Austrian force was on its own side of the Ticino, about one hundred miles to the east. Midway, in a direct line between the two armies, lay Turin, the capital of Sardinia. It was natural to suppose that the Austrians, after crossing the Ticino, would push at once for the city, and that the French would advance immediately to protect the position, already defended by a Sardinian army. But, after passing the Ticino, the Austrians marched but a few miles into Sardinia, though their force amounted to 120,000 men, at the invading point, with 100,000 reserve in Lombardy and Venice. It appeared easy for them to press on to the gates of Turin, because the country to be traversed was flat, and no strong fortresses were on the road. Instead of so proceeding, however, they diverged southwardly from the direct route to Turin, and reaching the river Sesia, began to erect fortifications on both banks of that stream. Here they were attacked by Sardinians, and fell back, but subsequently crossed the Sesia in force, and made a movement toward Turin. From the day of invasion to the 7th of May, more than a week elapsed before the Austrians approached the river Po. The Sardinians were engaged meantime in erecting defences on the route to Turin. They fortified both sides of the river Doro and neighboring highways, and were reinforced by French troops continually arriving. Meantime, as Sardinians abandoned the line of the Ticino, Austrians took their place, occupying parts of the flat country between Lake Maggiore and the left bank of the Sesia, below the town of Vercelli.

XXX.

One French army entered Italy by the Alpine Passes, near Mount Cenis, descending to the Doro, northwest of Turin; another was landed from steamers at Genoa, and sent up toward Turin by railroad. The railroad penetrates the Apennine hills of lower Piedmont, which are defended by strong Sardinian fortresses—Alessandria, Tortona, and Casale. It takes a northwesterly direction from Genoa up to Alessandria, and then branches westwardly to Turin. French detachments have been continually transported from the seaboard by this route, to join the land forces descending from the Alps. The entire French army became thus concentrated, with Sardinian auxiliaries in and about Turin, Susa and the Doro River. . . . . . . The Austrian invading army also divided—one force crossing the Ticino as noticed, another ascending east of that river to Lake Maggiore, and getting over into Upper Sardinia, at a point of the Ticino below that lake. The two hostile lines of battle, after a week's delay, occupied positions that were separated only by a few small rivers. The northern Austrian division rested at Arona, a place little more than a hundred miles north from Genoa, and less than half that distance north from Alessandria. The southern Austrian division rested in the neighborhood of Mortara, Vercelli, and Novara, three Sardinian towns, all within twenty miles of the Lombardo-Venetian border. The main Sardinian forces remained intrenched at Alessandria, and at Turin, the capital, about sixty miles distant.

XXXI.

It must be recollected that the country between Turin and the Ticino, above the line of Alessandria, is comparatively flat, with few obstacles to an advance on the capital. But below the line of Alessandria the mountain ranges begin, and break up Lower Sardinia or Piedmont down to the seacoast. The Austrians, in advancing on Turin, would leave this hilly country on their left flank, with all its strong fortresses and with a railroad bringing

French reinforcements constantly from Genoa. They would likewise advance in the face of a Sardinian army, defending the capital, and backed by a French army, marching down from the Alps. If, on the other hand, the Austrian commander-in-chief led his forces southward, he must meet a Sardinian army intrenched at Alessandria, and leave the upper French and Sardinian troops in his rear, either to pursue him, or to march into Austrian Italy, and stir up the people, already ripe for insurrection. It was a question that a general younger than Count Gyulai might have solved quickly by destroying the railroad east and south of Alessandria, and pushing boldly for Turin ; but such was not the immediate policy of that commander.

XXXII.

The fortified city of ALESSANDRIA is, perhaps, the strongest place in Piedmont. It is situated near the battle-ground of MARENGO. Its defences were constructed in the time of French possession, under Napoleon I., but the greater part of them were demolished after the peace of 1814. It was subsequently refortified, and again dismantled in 1835, but since that period has been repaired and strengthened more than ever. It contains a population of about 40,000 souls, beside the troops in camp. CASALE, on the river Po, and TORTONA, on the Scrivia, form right angles with Alessandria—the former north, the latter west. Both are strongly fortified. Casale contains a population of 22,000, Tortona, half that number. After passing below these strongholds, the first Italian battle-fields of Napoleon I., Montenotte, Millessimo, and Mondovi lie to the west, and Genoa to the south, through Apennine defiles.

XXXIII.

Should the Austrians fall back from their invasion, and recross the Ticino, they will have their own strongholds in Austrian Italy to defend. MILAN, capital of the Lombardo-Venetian kingdom, is a city of 162,000 inhabitants, with ramparts eight miles in circumference. MANTUA is another fortified city, 30,000 population, on an island of the river Mincio, and, like Milan, on a line of railway, branching to Venice and extending to Trieste. PIACENZA, near the Po, between Mantua and Sardinia, is a strong place, populous as Mantua, and walled around. VERONA, on the railway line and the river Adige, is looked upon as the key of northern Italy. It is walled and castellated, and has an intrenched camp, capable of harboring a large army, beside a general population of 50,000. VICENZA, a walled city, of between 30,000 and 40,000, and PADUA, another strongly-guarded city, with near 60,000 inhabitants, are both situated on the river Bacchiglione, at angles of the great railway line. BERGAMO and BRESCIA, are on the railway, between Verona and the capital, both well prepared for defence, and having each near 40,000 inhabitants. Reinforcements can be concentrated at any of these fortified points by means of railway branches, tapping Venice and Trieste of their recruits and army supplies.

XXXIV.

While the Austrian army delayed a week in the neighborhood of the Sesia ; while French troops were daily pouring into Sardinia from Genoa, south, and from the Alpine roads of Mount Cenis, on the west ; while nearly sixty thousand Sardinians were concentrating, with the French "army of Italy," near Susa ; while Alessandria, Casale, and Tortona were, meantime, defended by thirty thousand Piedmontese soldiers—other events were rapidly taking place in states.

bordering upon Sardinia. The Grand Duke of Tuscany, apprehensive of revolution, and sympathizing with Austria in the struggle, was urged by the principal inhabitants of Florence, his capital, to declare for Italian nationality, and side with Sardinia. This he refused to do. The people then assembled in mass, and demanded the grand duke's abdication. He was likewise averse to this ; but concluding that his personal safety was threatened, set off at once, with his family, and left the Tuscans to themselves. A provisional government was thereupon organized by the revolutionists, and Victor Emanuel, King of Sardinia, declared Protector of Tuscany. A Piedmontese commission was received, to govern in the name of Sardinia during the war. The grand duke and family proceeded, meantime, to Vienna, there to await a restoration by the Austrian army. . . . . . At Parma, about the same time, a revolutionary movement took place, and the duchess fled from the city, after naming a council of regency to preside over the state. The people formed a provisional government, and refused to acknowledge the regency. By some means, however, a counter-revolution was subsequently excited, assisted by the ducal troops in Parma. This turned the scale in favor of the regency. They succeeded in repressing the Sardinian sympathizers, and recalled the duchess to her government. . . . . . . At Rome, where French troops have so long been stationed, and in other cities of the Papal States, demonstrations were made in favor of the Italian national cause, but no changes of local government were attempted. Several Austrian columns invaded the Papal States bordering on the Adriatic. . . . . . The Arch-Duke Maximilian, who was viceroy of the Lombardo-Venetian kingdom before hostilities commenced, was summoned to Vienna, after the passage of the Ticino. Gen. Gyulai, commander-in-chief of the Austrian army, took the position of governor-general, in place of the archduke, and at once placed Venice, Verona, and other Austrio-Italian cities under martial law, to prevent any rising of their inhabitants in favor of Sardinia. In this manner Austria found herself compelled to watch open and secret opponents, and to take every step forward as though treading on an explosive mine.

XXXV.

It was generally believed, by Austrians as well as French, that a secret revolutionary understanding existed throughout all the Italian States, including Austrian Italy and the kingdom of Naples ; and that a secret society, La Giovane Italia, or " Young Italy," organized in 1830, of which Mazzini, Manin, Garribaldi, and other Italians were members, had kept up its connections, under modified forms, since that year, and was covertly protected by Victor Emanuel, under favor of Napoleon III. The discipline and system of this revolutionary fraternity were alleged to be perfect. Supplies of arms, long accumulating, were said to be buried at convenient localities, and the patriotic members awaited only a proper time to rise in all parts of Italy. A manifesto was published in the French journals, purporting to be signed by Garribaldi, to the chiefs of the National Society in various states. It read as follows :

"To the National Society of Italy :

"In the present state of Italian affairs, the President considers it his duty to transmit to the Society the following secret instructions :

"1. No sooner have hostilities commenced between Piedmont and Austria, than you will at once rise in insurrection to the cry of ' Viva l'Italia e Vittorio Emmanuele—Out with the Austrians !'

"2. If insurrection should be impossible in your own town, all young men able to bear arms will leave it, and proceed to the nearest town where insurrection has been already successful, or is likely to be so. Among neighboring towns you will choose those nearest to Piedmont, where all Italian forces should be concentrated.

"3. You will make every effort to vanquish and disorganize the Austrian army, intercepting its communications, destroying its bridges and telegraphs, burning all depots of provisions or clothing, and making prisoners of all important persons in the Austrian service.

"4. Do not at first fire on Italian or Hungarian soldiers, but, on the contrary, endeavor to induce them to follow your own flag, and receive with open arms all who give way to your exhortations.

"5. Regular troops who will embarrass the national cause will be at once sent into Piedmont.

"6. Wherever the insurrection is successful, the man who stands highest in the popular estimation will assume military and civil authority, with the title of Provisional Commissioner for King Victor Emanuel, and will maintain it until the arrival of the Commissioner dispatched by the Piedmontese government.

"7. The Provisional Commissioner will abolish the taxes on bread, corn, etc., and in general all taxes which do not exist in Sardinian territory.

"8. A levy will at once be made, by means of conscription, of young men from 18 to 20 years of age, in the proportion of 10 to 1,000 of the gross population. All men also, from 20 to 35, willing to bear arms in defence of the national independence, may be received as volunteers, both conscripts and volunteers being at once dispatched to Piedmont.

"9. The Provisional Commissioner will appoint a council of war, with power to try and punish, within 24 hours, all who may be guilty of crimes against the national cause, or against the life or property of pacific citizens. The council will make no distinctions of rank or class, but no person may be punished for crimes committed anterior to the insurrection.

"10. He will not allow of the establishment of political journals, but he will publish a bulletin of all facts which it is necessary to make public.

"11. He will dismiss from their posts all magistrates or officers who may be opposed to the new order of things, always proceeding with prudence and caution.

"12. He will maintain the severest discipline, applying to all the laws suitable during a time of war. He will be inexorable to deserters, and will give the strictest orders on this subject to all his subordinates.

"13. He will send to King Victor Emanuel a precise description of the arms, ammunition and money found in the various towns and provinces, and he will await commands on this subject.

"14. In case of necessity he will make requisitions for money, horses, carts, shops, etc., always giving a corresponding receipt; but he will punish with the utmost rigor all who shall make requisitions of this kind without the most pressing necessity, or without making a definite contract.

"15. Until the time referred to in the first article of these instructions, you will use every means in your power for manifesting the aversion which Italy feels for the Austrian domination and for the governments dependent on Austria, as well as her love for independence and her confidence in the house of Savoy and the Piedmontese government ; but you will do all in your power to prevent untimely or isolated movements.

"For the President,
"The Vice-President GARRIBALDI.

"TURIN, *March* 1."

XXXVI.

The grounds wherein the Austrian Government took the initiative of the war were set forth, at length, in two official documents. The first was a manifesto, from the Emperor Francis Joseph himself, declaring war, and the second a circular of Count Buol, Austrian prime-minister, addressed to diplomatic agents of his government, residing at foreign courts. The " Imperial Manifesto " is as follows ; proclaimed in Vienna and throughout all Austrian territory :

"TO MY PEOPLE.

"I have ordered my faithful and gallant army to put a stop to the inimical acts which for a series of years have been committed by the neighboring State of Sardinia against the indisputable rights of my Crown, and against the integrity of the realm placed by God under my care, which acts have lately attained the very highest point. By so doing I have fulfilled the painful but unavoidable duty of a Sovereign. My conscience being at rest, I can look up to an omnipotent God, and patiently await his award. With confidence I leave my decision to the impartial judgment of contemporaneous and future generations. Of the approbation of my faithful subjects I am sure. More than ten years ago that same enemy—violating international law and the usages of war, and without any offence being given—entered the Lombardo-Venetian territory with the intention of acquiring possession of it. Although the enemy was twice totally defeated by my gallant army, and at the mercy of the victor, I behaved generously, and proposed a reconciliation. I did not appropriate to myself one inch of his territory, I encroached on no right which belongs to the Crown of Sardinia, as one of the members of the European family of nations. I insisted on no guaranties against the recurrence of similar events. The hand of peace which I in all sincerity extended, and which was taken, appeared to me to be a sufficient guaranty. The blood which my army shed for the honor and right of Austria I sacrificed on the altar of peace. The reward for such unexampled forbearance was an immediate continuation of enmity, which increased from year to year, and perfidious agitation against the peace and welfare of my Lombardo-Venetian kingdom. Well knowing what a precious boon peace was for my people and for Europe, I patiently bore with these new hostilities. My patience was not exhausted when the more extensive measures which I was forced to take, in consequence of the revolutionary agitation on the frontiers of my Italian provinces and within the same, were made an excuse for a higher degree of hostility. Willingly accepting the well-meant mediation of friendly Powers for the maintenance of peace, I consented to become a party to a Congress of the five great Powers. The four points proposed by the Royal Government of Great Britain as a basis for the deliberations of the Congress were forwarded to my Cabinet, and I accepted them, with the conditions which were calculated to bring about a true, sincere, and durable peace. In the consciousness that no step on the part of my Government could, even in the most remote degree, lead to a disturbance of the peace, I demanded that the Power which was the cause of the complication and had brought about the danger of war, should, as a preliminary measure, disarm. Being pressed thereto by friendly Powers, I at length accepted the proposal for a general disarmament. The mediation failed in consequence of the unacceptableness of the conditions on which Sardinia made her consent dependent. Only one means of maintaining peace remained. I addressed myself directly to the Sardinia Government, and summoned it to place its army on a peace footing and to disband the free corps. As Sar. dinia did not accede to my demand the moment for deciding the matter by an appeal to arms has arrived. I have ordered my army to enter Sardinia. I am aware of the vast importance of the measure, and if ever my duties as a monarch weighed heavily on me it is at this moment. War is the scourge of mankind. I see with sorrow that the lives and property of thousands of my subjects are imperilled, and deeply feel what a severe trial war is for my realm, which, being occupied with its internal development, greatly requires the continuance of peace. But the heart of the Monarch must be silent at the command of honor and duty. On the frontiers is an armed enemy, who, in alliance with the revolutionary party, openly announces his intention to obtain possession of the dependencies of Austria in Italy. To support him, the ruler over France —who under futile pretexts interferes in the legally established relations of the Italian Peninsula—has set his troops in movement. Detachments of them have already crossed the frontiers of Sardinia. The crown which I received without spot or blemish from my forefathers has already seen trying times. The glorious history of our country gives evidence that Providence, when there is a foreshadowing that the greatest good of humanity is in danger of being overthrown in Europe, has frequently used the sword of Austria in order to dispel that shadow. We are again on the eve of such a period. The over. throw of the things that be is not only aimed at by factions, but by Thrones. The sword which I have been forced to draw is sanctified, inasmuch as it is a defence for the honor and rights of all peoples and States, and for all that is held most dear by humanity. To you, my people, whose devotion to the hereditary reigning family may serve as a model for all the nations of the earth, I now address myself. In the conflict which has commenced you will stand by me with your oft-proved fidelity and devotion. To your sons, whom I have taken into the ranks of the army, I, their commander, send my martial greeting. With pride you may regard them, for the eagle of Austria will, with their support, soar high. Our struggle is a just one and we begin it with courage and confidence. We hope, however, that we shall not stand alone in it. The soil on which he have to do battle was made fruitful by the blood lost by our German brethren when they won those bulwarks which they have maintained up to the present day. There the crafty enemies of Germany have generally begun their game when they have wished to break her internal power. The feeling that such a danger is now imminent prevails in all parts of Germany, from the hut to the throne, from one frontier to the other. I speak as a sovereign member of the Germanic Confederation when I call attention to the common danger, and recall to memory the glorious times in which Europe had to thank the general and fervent enthusiasm of Germany for its liberation.

" For God and fatherland !

" Given at my residence and metropolis of Vienna on the 28th day of April, 1859.

" FRANCIS JOSEPH."

XXXVII.

Count Buol, in behalf of the government, subsequently made public his dispatches to the various diplomatic agents of Austria. In connection with the " Imperial Manifesto," it becomes the efficient statement of Austria's posi- tion as a party to the war. It is as follows :

" TO THE AUSTRIAN DIPLOMATIC AGENTS, ETC., (INCLOSING THE EMPEROR'S MANIFESTO, APRIL 29, 1859.

" "I send herewith a copy of the manifesto which the emperor, our master, has this day addressed to his peo- ple. His majesty announces to the empire that he has resolved to order the Austrian army to cross the Ticino. The Cabinet had accepted the last proposition of mediation of Great Britain, but our adversaries have not followed that example, and we have accordingly submitted to arms the defence of our cause. At this solemn moment it is my duty to explain once again to our representatives abroad the circum- stances against the fatal power of which have failed all the attempts made to maintain European peace, which has been so long and so happily preserved.

" The Court of Turin, in returning an evasive reply to our summons to disarm, has only given one more proof of the same hostility which for too long a time already has had the triple and unfortunate privilege of combating the sacred rights of Austria, disquieting Europe, and encouraging the hopes of revolution. As this hostility could not be broken down by the forbearance of Austria, the empire was at last under the ne- cessity of having recourse to arms.

"Austria has tranquilly supported a long series of offences from an enemy weaker than herself, because she knows that her high mission is to preserve as long as possible the peace of the world ; because the emperor and his people know and love the labors of a progressive pacific development, which leads to a higher degree of prosperity. But no man of just mind and of upright heart can now doubt the right which Austria has to make war on Piedmont.

" Piedmont has never sincerely accepted the treaty by which, ten years ago, she promised at Milan to live in peace and friendship with Austria. Twice beaten in war, which had been caused by her mad pretensions, and although she had been cruelly punished, that State still maintains her former views with a deplorable tenacity. The son of Charles Albert appears passionately to desire the day when the inheritance of his house, which had been restored to him in its integrity by the moderation and magnanimity of Austria, should be for the third time made the stake of a game disastrous to the world.

" The ambition of a dynasty whose vain pretensions touching the future welfare of Italy are neither justified by the nature nor by the history of that country, has not hesitated to form an unnatural alliance with revo- lution. Deaf to all warnings, it has surrounded itself with the malcontents of all the States of Italy, and the hopes of all the enemies of the legitimate government of the Italian peninsula have found their chief support at Turin. A criminal abuse has been made of the national feelings of the Italian people. Endea- vors have been made to keep up and encourage disturbances in Italy, in order that Piedmont might have a pretext for hypocritically deploring the state of Italy, and assuming in the eyes of short-sighted and senseless people the part of a liberator.

"To assist in this rash undertaking, an unbridled press every day endeavored to carry beyond the frontiers of the neighboring States a moral insurrection against the order of legitimate things. This state of things no country in Europe could tolerate without exposing itself in the end to deep and dangerous excitement.

Out of love for those hollow dreams of the future, and in order to secure to herself support from abroad, Piedmont took part in a war in which she had no concern againt a foreign power, and sacrificed her soldiers for a foreign object. She was also seen at the Conferences of Paris, with a presumption quite affronting to the governments of Italy, her own country—governments which had never offended her.

" But, that nobody might believe these wild desires and efforts were associated with the smallest sentiments in favor of the peaceful prosperity of Italy, the angry passions of Sardinia redoubled whenever any of the Sovereigns of Italy followed the inspiration of indulgence and conciliation, and whenever the emperor Francis Joseph gave signal proofs of his love for his Italian subjects, of his solicitude for the happiness and progress of the richest and most favored countries of Italy.

" When their Imperial Majesties visited the Italian provinces, receiving the homage of their faithful subjects, and marking every step by conferring a host of benefits, the journals of Turin were allowed freely to advocate regicide.

" When the emperor intrusted the administration of Lombardy and Venice to the Archduke Ferdinand Maximilian, his brother, a prince endowed with high intelligence, animated by liberal and kindly intentions, and profoundly sympathizing with the true spirit of the Italian people, no pains were spared at Turin to cause the prince's noble intentions to be repaid with as much ingratitude as could be produced in the midst of a well-disposed nation by odious instigations incessantly repeated.

" The Court of Turin, having once entered upon the path in which the only choice was either to follow the revolution or take the lead, could not but more and more lose the power and the will to observe the laws which regulate the relations of independent States, or even to recognize any of the limits imposed by the law of nations on the conduct of all civilized States. Under the most frivolous pretexts, Sardinia declares herself liberated from the obligations clearly imposed by treaties, as proved by the conventions with Austria and the Italian States for the extradition of criminals and deserters. Her emissaries overrun the neighboring States, exciting soldiers to disobey their chiefs; treading under foot all the rules of military discipline, Piedmont admitted deserters in the ranks of her own army.

" Such were the acts of a government which boasts its civilizing mission, and in whose states there are journalists whose journals find readers, and who, not content with simply making an apology for assassination, count their bleeding victims with fiendish joy.

" Who, after this, can any longer doubt that that government regarded as the chief obstacle the rights which Austria derives from treaties, and accordingly sought to get rid of them by all the means of a dishonest policy? The true intentions of Piedmont, which had long ceased to be a secret to any one, were openly avowed as soon as that State was sufficiently assured of foreign assistance, and had no further necessity for concealing its projects of war and revolution. Europe, which sees in the respect of existing treaties the palladium of its repose, received with well-merited disfavor a declaration containing the assertion that Sardinia considered herself attacked by Austria because Austria would not relinquish the exercise of the rights and duties conferred by treaties—because she maintained her right to keep a garrison in Piacenza, a right guaranteed by the great Powers of Europe; and because she presumed to form alliances with other Sovereigns of the Italian peninsula for the common defence of their legitimate interests. There remained but one other pretext, and that was alleged accordingly. The cabinet of Turin declares that all remedies for the state of Italy would be merely palliatives as long as the Austrian dominion extends over the Italian soil. This is an open attack on the territorial possessions of Austria, exceeding the limit to which a power like Austria could tolerate the provocations of a less powerful state without an appeal to arms. Such is, stripped of the tissue of falsehoods with which it was enveloped, the truth respecting the line of conduct which for ten years past the House of Savoy has followed, at the suggestion of unprincipled advisers. It should be said, also, that the accusations and reproaches by which the Sardinian cabinet endeavors to present under a false light its attacks on Austria are nothing but wicked calumnies.

" Austria is a conservative power, with whom religion, morality, and historical right are sacred. She knows how to estimate, to protect, and to weigh in the scale of equality what is noble and legitimate in the national spirit of nations. Her extensive dominions consist of different races, of different languages ; the emperor embraces them all in the same love, and their union under the sceptre of our august dynasty is advantageous to the whole of the great family of European nations; but the pretensions of forming new States, according to the limits of nationalities, is the most dangerous of all Utopian schemes.

" To put forward such a pretension is to break with history; and to seek to carry it into execution in any point of Europe is to shake to its foundations the firmly organized order of States, and to threaten the Continent with subversion and chaos. Europe feels this, and she attaches herself the more firmly to the territorial divisions fixed by the Congress of Vienna at the close of an epoch of continental wars, with as much regard as possible to historical conditions. There is not a power whose possessions are more legitimate than those in Italy restored to the House of Hapsburg by the Congress which reëstablished the kingdom of Sardinia, and made it the brilliant present of Genoa.

" Lombardy has been for centuries a fief of the empire of Germany ; Venice was given to Austria in exchange for her giving up her Belgian provinces. Thus, therefore, what the cabinet of Turin calls the true reason of the discontent of the inhabitants of Lombardo-Venetia, showing thereby itself the utter want of foundation for its other alleged grievances, namely the domination of Austria on the Po and on the Adriatic., is a solid and unquestionable right in every respect, and one which the Austrian eagles will preserve from all attack. But it is not only a legitimate government—it is a just and benevolent one, which administers the Lombardo-Venetian provinces. Those beautiful countries have prospered more rapidly than could have been hoped after the long and painful years of revolution ; Milan and several other celebrated towns display wealth worthy of their history; Venice is recovering from her profound decline, and displaying new life ; the administration of justice is regular, manufactures and commerce prosper, science and art are cultivated with ardor. The public burdens are not heavier than in other parts of the monarchy; they would even be lighter if the fatal effects of Sardinian policy did not require that the State should augment its forces, and consequently raise new revenues. The great majority of the people of Lombardy and Venetia are content; the number of the discontented who have forgotten the lessons of 1848 is small in comparison ; and it would be less without the incessant excitations of Piedmont.

" Piedmont, therefore, does not trouble herself about populations which are suffering and oppressed; but she rather interrupts a regular state of things, and the development of future prosperity. Human prudence cannot foresee how long this deplorable enterprise will trouble the peace of Italy, but a terrible responsibility weighs on those who have wickedly and deliberately exposed their country and Europe to new catastrophes.

" The revolution so carefully kept alive in all the peninsula, has promptly followed the impulse given it. A military rising has taken place at Florence—it has compelled his Imperial Highness the Duke of Tuscany, to leave his states. Insurrection reigns at Massa and Carrara, under the protection of Sardinia.

" But France, which for a long time past, we repeat, has shared that terrible moral responsibility—France has hastened by acts to assume it altogether. The government of the Emperor of the French caused, on the

26th of this month, his *Chargé d'Affaires* at Vienna to declare that he should consider the passage of the Ticino by the Austrian troops as a declaration of war against France. While we were still waiting at Vienna for the reply of Piedmont to the summons to disarm, France caused her troops to enter Sardinia by the land and sea frontiers knowing well that by so doing she placed in the balance, the weight which would carry the last resolutions of the court of Turin.

" And why, we ask, were the legitimate hopes of the friends of peace in Europe thus to be annihilated by a single blow? Because the time had arrived at which projects long meditated in silence have arrived at maturity—at which the second French Empire desires to give substance to *its ideas*—at which the political state of Europe, based on right, is to be sacrificed to its legitimate pretensions—at which the treaties which form the basis of public European power are to be replaced by *political wisdom* which the power that rules at Paris has announced to the astonished world.

" The traditions of the first Napoleon are resumed. Such is the signification of the struggle on the eve of which Europe is placed.

" May the world, undeceived, be penetrated with this conviction—that now, as half a century ago, the question at stake is to defend the independence of states, and to protect the most precious possessions of nations against ambition and the spirit of domination.

" The Emperor Francis Joseph, the chief of our empire, although he deplores the evils which will be occasioned by the impending war, has confidently placed his just cause in the hands of Divine Providence. He has drawn the sword because guilty hands have attacked the dignity and honor of his crown; he will fight with the profound sentiment of his right, strong in the enthusiasm and courage of his people, accompanied by the wishes of all those whose conscience distinguishes truth from falsehood, right from injustice.

" You will communicate to the government to which you have the honor to be accredited, both the Imperial manifesto and the present dispatch. Accept, etc."

XXXVIII.

Simultaneously with the issue of his war proclamation, the Austrian Emperor invested Count General GYULAI, with full powers to carry it into effect by an invasion of Sardinian territory. He dispatched the following order to that General :

" FELDZEUGMEISTER COUNT GYULAI—

" After fruitless attempts to secure peace for my empire, without compromising its dignity, I am necessitated to have recourse to arms.

" With confidence I confide the rights of Austria to the best hands—to the hands of a tried and gallant army.

" Your fidelity and bravery, your exemplary discipline, the justice of the cause which you defend, and a glorious past, guaranty to me your success.

" Soldiers of the Second Army ! it is for you to secure victory to the spotless flag of Austria. Take with you into battle the blessing of God and the confidence of your emperor.

" FRANCIS JOSEPH."

On receipt of this order, the new Austrian Governor-General of the Lombardo-Venetian Kingdom, issued his own proclamation to the inhabitants of that country as follows :

" TO THE PEOPLE OF LOMBARDY AND VENETIA.

" The provocations given to the Imperial Government by a bold faction of the Sardinian States, an enemy to all order and right, and its obstinacy in rejecting all overtures of peace and moderation, have exhausted the generous patience of our august emperor and master, and made him resolve to protect the cause of justice and right, and make it triumph by the force of arms. Intrusted by the sovereign will, with the chief command of the army, the powers of the civil and military governments of the Lombardo-Venetian Kingdom are, by order of his majesty, concentrated in my hands during the war, from the moment the imperial eagles and our glorious standard shall have reached the Piedmontese territory. The readiness with which your young men have left your flourishing fields to hasten under the imperial colors, the goodwill with which you have provided for the wants of our brave army, the universal feeling of personal duty, all assure me that tranquillity and public order will be maintained, notwithstanding the perfidious suggestions of the subversive party. In order to protect you in case it were disturbed by some madman, a sufficient force will remain among you to maintain the public peace ; and he shall have cause to repent who, by any means whatsoever, may attempt to disturb it, and to increase the sufferings of his country. Justice, respect for the laws, obedience to the authorities—such has always been my motto.

On passing the Ticino, and entering upon Piedmontese territory, the Austrian general issued a second proclamation, addressed to Victor Emanuel's subjects :

" TO THE PEOPLE OF SARDINIA.

" In crossing your frontiers, it is not against you, people of Sardinia, that we direct our arms ; but against a small destructive party, powerful by its boldness, which oppresses you by its violence, rejects all offers of peace, attacks the rights of the other Italian States, and even those of Austria. The Imperial eagles, if you salute them on their arrival without anger and without resistance, will bring you order, tranquillity, moderation ; and the peaceable citizen may be assured that liberty, honor, the laws and property shall be respected and protected as inviolable and sacred things. The constant discipline which, in the imperial troops, is equal to their valor, is a guaranty for my word. Interpreting to you the generous sentiments of my august emperor and master, I, while treading your soil, proclaim and repeat that this war is intended neither against the people nor against the nation, but against a subversive party, which, under the specious mask of liberty, would deprive the whole world of it, if the God of armies was not also the God of nations. When your adversary and ours shall have been vanquished, when order and peace shall have been restored, you, who may now call us your enemies, will soon consider us your liberators and friends.''

XXXIX.

On receiving intelligence of the invasion of Sardinian territory by Austrian troops, the Emperor Napoleon III. issued his manifesto, which was at once proclaimed in Paris, and throughout France :

MANIFESTO OF NAPOLEON III.

" Austria, by ordering the entry of her army into the territories of the King of Sardinia, our ally, has declared war against us. She thus violates treaties and justice, and menaces our frontiers. All the great Powers have protested against this act of aggression. Piedmont having accepted the conditions which ought to have insured peace, one asks what can be the reason of this sudden invasion? It is because Austria has driven matters to such an extremity, that her dominion must either extend to the Alps, or Italy must be free to the shores of the Adriatic—for every corner of Italy which remains independent, endangers the power of Austria. Hitherto moderation has been the rule of my conduct, but now energy becomes my first duty. France must now to arms, and resolutely tell Europe—' I wish not for conquest, but I am determined firmly to maintain my national and traditional policy. I observe treaties on condition that they are not violated against me. I respect the territories and the rights of neutral Powers, but I boldly avow my sympathies with a people whose history is mingled with our own, and who now groan under foreign oppression.' France has shown her hatred of anarchy. Her will was to give me power sufficiently strong to reduce into subjection abettors of disorder and the incorrigible members of old factions, who are incessantly seen concluding compacts with our enemies, but she has not for that purpose abandoned her civilizing character. Her natural allies have always been those who desire the amelioration of the human race, and when she draws the sword it is not to govern but to free. The object, then, of this war is to restore Italy to herself, not to impose upon her a change of masters, and we shall then have upon our frontiers a friendly people, who will owe to us their independence. We do not enter Italy to foment disorder, or to disturb the power of the Holy Father, whom we replaced upon his throne, but to remove from him his foreign pressure, which burdens the whole peninsula, and to help to establish there order based upon lawful satisfied interests. In fine, then, we enter this classic ground, rendered illustrious by so many victories, to seek the footsteps of our fathers. God grant that we may be worthy of them. I am about to place myself at the head of the army. I leave in France the empress and my son. Seconded by the experience and the enlightenment of the emperor's last surviving brother, she will understand how to show herself worthy of the grandeur of her mission. I confide them to the valor of the army which remains in France to keep watch upon our frontiers and to protect our homes. I confide them to the patriotism of the National Guard. I confide them, in a word, to the entire people, who will encircle them with that affection and devotedness of which I daily receive so many proofs. Courage, then, and union! Our country is again about to show the world that she has not degenerated. Providence will bless our efforts, for that cause is holy in the eyes of God which rests on justice, humanity, love of country, and independence.''

After issue of this war-proclamation, the Emperor Napoleon III. made immediate preparations to proceed to the seat of war, as commander-in-chief of the armies. The title of his army already in Sardinia, was changed from " Army of the Alps" to " Army of Italy"—the name which his uncle's victories had rendered glorious. He took measures at once for the government of France during his absence, by issuing the following decrees establishing a provisional Regency :

FIRST IMPERIAL DECREE.

'' NAPOLEON, by the Grace of God and the national will Emperor of the French, to all present and future greeting :

" Wishing to give to our beloved wife, the empress, the marks of high confidence we place in her,

" And considering that it is our intention to assume the command of the army of Italy, we have resolved to confer, as we confer by these presents, upon our well-beloved wife, the empress, the title of Regent, to exercise the functions of the same during our absence, in conformity with our instructions and our orders, such as we shall have made known in the General Order of the service which we shall establish, and which shall be inscribed in the Great Book of the State.

" Let it be understood that cognizance shall be given to our uncle, Prince Jerome, to the Presidents of the great bodies of the State, to the members of our Privy Council, and to the Ministers, of such orders and instructions ; and that in no case can the empress deviate from their tenor in the exercise of the functions of Regent.

" It is our wish that the empress should preside, in our name, at the Privy Council and at the Council of Ministers. However, it is not our intention that the Empress Regent should authorize by her signature the promulgation of any *senatus-consultum*, or any law of the State other than those which are actually pending before the Senate, the Legislative Body, and the Council of State, referring ourselves in this respect to the orders and instructions above mentioned.

" We charge our Minister of State to give communication of the present letters patent to the Senate, which will have them registered, and to our Keeper of the Seals, Minister of Justice, who will have them published in the *Bulletin des Lois*.

" Given at the Palace of the Tuileries, this 3d of May, 1859.   " NAPOLEON.
(Countersigned)   " ACHILLE FOULD, Minister of State."

SECOND IMPERIAL DECREE.

"Napoleon, by the Grace of God and the national will, Emperor of the French, to all who may see these presents greeting:

"On the point of starting to take command of the army of Italy, we have by our letters patent of this day confided the Regency to our well-beloved wife, the empress, and we have regulated for the time of our absence the order of service by an act inserted in the State archives, and made known to our uncle, Prince Jerome Napoleon, to the members of the Privy Council, to the Presidents of the Senate, of the Legislative Body, and of the Council of State.

"Desirous of giving to our uncle, Prince Jerome, marks of the high confidence we place in him, and by the aid of his intelligence, experience and devotion to our person to facilitate the task of our well-beloved wife, we have decided and do decide that the Empress Regent shall take, on the resolutions and decrees which may be submitted to her, the counsel of the Prince, our uncle. We have, moreover, conferred on him, as we confer on him by these presents, the right of presiding, in the absence of the Empress Regent, at the Privy Council and at the Council of Ministers.

"Given at the Palace of the Tuileries, this 3d of May, 1859.

                                             "Napoleon.

                (Countersigned)   "Achille Fould,

                                         "Minister of State."

The next official proclamation of importance was that issued by Marshal Canrobert, French General in Sardinia, from his headquarters at Alessandria, between Genoa and Turin. Its concluding sentences to the army were as follows—indicating in some degree a line of operations to which the concentration of troops was tending :

"Soldiers! the precipitate march which you have just made across the Alps has not allowed the solicitude of the emperor's government to supply you with all of which you stand in need. You will soon receive it You must call to mind that the warriors, our forefathers, who have preceded us in these fine countries, were in want of everything at the time that they covered the flag of France and the country with immortal glory The great French army will soon find itself opposite the Austrian army. They are old acquaintances. Both have seen each other at Lodi, at Arcole, at Marengo, and at Wagram—illustrious names, which you will soon cause to be followed by others equally glorious."

Having reached this stage of warlike progress, we may seek, in other quarters, the original cause of the dynastic struggle apparently impending.

RETROSPECT OF WARS AND TREATIES.

I.

Understanding the present official position of hostile sovereigns, the relative localities of armies, the character of country forming the seat of war, and the defensive and offensive resources on either side, we await further movements of the belligerent forces, and meantime turn to inquire concerning the merits and causes of the great impending war. To arrive at just conclusions upon the matter, it will be best to view it in the light of historical facts ; and we may, therefore, glance briefly at an immediate sequence of events which marked the era of the French Revolution, immediately preceding the extraordinary rise of Napoleon the First. To do this, we go back to the last century, and to a period when the French Revolution broke out with a violence that deluged France in blood, and swept away its own first leaders. There were then on the principal thrones of Europe, some half-dozen families, more or less connected by ties of relationship, or diplomatic policy, and classified as follows :

France.—Louis XVI. (*Bourbon*), Marie Antoinette (*House of Austria*).
England.—George III. (*Brunswick—Hanover*).

HOLLAND.—William V.
SPAIN.—Charles IV. (*Bourbon*).
PRUSSIA.—Frederick William III. (*Hohenzollern*).
NAPLES.—Ferdinand IV. (*Bourbon*).
PORTUGAL.—Maria [widow of Peter], (*Braganza*).
RUSSIA.—Paul I. (*Holstein—Gatthorp*).
AUSTRIA.—Francis II. (*Austria—Lorraine*).
SWEDEN.—Gustavus IV. (*Holstein—Entin*).
DENMARK.—Christian VI. (*Holstein—Gluckstaudt*).
SARDINIA.—Victor Emanuel III. (*Arragon*).

By this table we see that the chief domination in Europe was enjoyed by a few families, connected by traditions, policy, and blood. The numberless inferior sovereignties into which the European continent was cut up, were all more or less dependent upon the powerful dynasties, and guided by their influence. Urged, at various times, by dynastic ambition, these monarchs, and their predecessors, had usurped rule and appropriated territory whenever they could do so without danger to their own safety. By constant encroachments upon weaker neighbors, some of the more powerful kingdoms had absorbed large districts of country to which they held no other right but that of conquest and spoliation. Others had extended their dominions through royal marriages, and others found themselves enriched by bequest of neighboring sovereigns, who died without legitimate heirs. Poland had been despoiled by Russia ; Prussia had been enlarged at the expense of a neighbor, by dividing Friesland, and she had invaded Holland to change its form of government. Austria had sequestrated Bohemian, Polish, Italian, Hungarian, and French territory. During the eighteenth century, Europe had been convulsed by wars of dynastic succession, and before its termination the remaining years were yet to record a fearful list of five emperors and five kings assassinated, five governments overturned, six sovereigns discrowned, and one kingdom blotted entirely from the political map of Europe. It was destined within a single decade before its close, to behold a lieutenant of artillery rise to be a conquering Cæsar, deposing five monarchs and enthroning eight, whilst his subordinate instruments were subjugating a mighty continent. But, as yet unconscious of the volcano which labored under the crust of established things, the potentates of Europe feasted, married, made laws, and broke treaties, according to policy or convenience. Upon such a state of politics the French Revolution cast out its turbulent theories and facts, as from a fierce volcanic upheaval.

II.

The policy of the French Revolution was declared by its leaders to be the propagandism of democratic ideas. The coalition of Austria and Prussia, with the *refugee* French Noblesse, avowedly to protect the Bourbon dynasty, provoked the first marked violence of democracy in France, and led to the regicide of Louis XVI. and his queen, and the sanguinary reign of Robespierre, Marat, Danton, and their confederates. In January, 1793, Great Britain joined the European dynastic movement against revolutionary France, and subsequently dispatched an army to the Netherlands, to check an advance of French armies in that quarter of the continent. About the same time, the strongly-fortified town of Toulon, in France, was surrendered to England by its inhabitants, who remained loyal to the Bourbon cause. At this period Robespierre was infusing his energy into the republican government, and vigorous measures were taken to increase and discipline the revolutionary armies. Several victories were successively gained by French commanders over hostile armies. The Legitimist allies were driven out of the Netherlands in 1794, and Holland organized into the "Batavian Republic," under French control. Prussia became dispirited, and drew off her troops, and in the following year Great Britain commenced a negotiation for peace, which was soon broken off by the refusal of France to restore Belgium to Austria.

III.

Meanwhile, since Louis XVI. died by the guillotine, on the 21st January, 1793, a civil warfare raged between royalists and republicans in France. Napoléon Bonaparte had distinguished himself by the capture of Toulon from the Legitimists ; and Marie Antoinette had been decapitated, like her husband. In July, 1794, Robespierre, Couthon, St. Just, and others of the Conventional Government, were assassinated. Their fall ended the Reign of Terror, which was followed, in 1795, by the establishment of a Directory of five men, a Senate of two hundred and fifty, and a Council of five hundred members. From the beginning of the Revolution, its actors had sworn "hatred to kings and royalty, and that no foreign power should ever be suffered to dictate laws to the French." They had also declared it to be settled French policy, "to assist all nations desirous of recovering their liberty." In this propagandistic spirit, five armies had conquered Savoy and the Italian province of Nice, on the border ; had reduced Belgium and the Netherlands, and overrun German territory to the Rhine ; thirteen levies being raised in succession, and victories gained over Hanoverians, English, Dutch, Austrians, and Prussians. In 1795–6, France and the Netherlands united to oppose the alliance of Austria, England, and Russia. General Bonaparte was sent to Italy by the Directory, and gained the victories of Montenotte, Millésimo, Lodi, Arcola, Rivoli, and others, in less than one year. He pushed through Lombardy, and captured TRIESTE. In Italy he established two republics—the Ligurian or Genoese, and the Cisalpine or Milanese. He invaded independent Venice, changed her government, and then, at the Peace of Campo Formio, gave that republic up to Austria. After his Italian campaigns, Bonaparte was sent with an army to Egypt, and returning in 1797 to France, was made commander-in-chief of her armies. Seizing his opportunity, on the 9th November (18th Brumaire), he overturned the Directory of Five, by the assistance of his brother Lucien, President of the Council of Five Hundred, which body was dissolved at the bayonet's point. A new constitution was then adopted, and three CONSULS chosen as heads of the French Republic. Barras, Siéyès, and Bonaparte were the Consuls, but Bonaparte was intrusted with chief powers, and took the field as general. He led another army into Italy, and gained the battle of Marengo, on the wide plain between ALESSANDRIA and TORTONA, in the neighborhood which the Austrians under Gyulai lately penetrated after crossing the Ticino. On his return to Paris, many conspiracies were formed against the First Consul, but he succeeded in making himself almost a dictator in government. In 1801, he concluded treaties with the United States, Austria, Naples, the Pope, Bavaria, Portugal, Russia, and Turkey, and finally the Peace of Amiens in 1802 with England. France then found herself at peace with all the world, after having established the Batavian Republic in Holland, and the Italian Republic, with Bonaparte as President, beyond the Alps. The French nation then extended Bonaparte's term as Consul ten years, and finally the question of his *Consul-*

ship for life was submitted to the nation, and decided in the affirmative by 3,368,259 against 209,626 votes. At this time the territory of France had increased, by conquest and negotiation, some 42,000 square miles. In 1803, France mediated in German affairs, settled difficulties in Switzerland, annexed Elba and Parma. The next year beheld a new war with England, and Bonaparte took upon himself the imperial dignity. Napoleon I. was thus *Emperor* of France and *President* of the Italian Republic. This being contradictory, he crowned himself with the iron crown of Lombardy at Milan, and made his stepson, Eugene Beauharnais, Viceroy of Italy, thus abolishing the republic. Genoa, Parma, Piacenza, and Guastalla were also incorporated with France. Napoleon I. gave the small republic of Lucca as a principality to Felix Bacciocchi, who had served him. These usurpations and encroachments of the French Imperial Government alarmed all Europe, and in 1805, treaties were concluded between Russia, England, Austria, Spain, and Sweden, by which those powers combined against France, with secret understanding, to dismember her swollen possessions in case of triumph. The object of the coalition, as stated, was "to compel the French Government to agree to the reestablishment of peace and the *equilibrium of Europe.*"

IV.

Now commenced the struggle; on the part of Napoleon I. to carry into effect his own ideas of a Continental System; and on the side of allied Europe to restore the continent to the position it occupied previous to French Revolution. The Treaty of St. Petersburg, between Russia and Great Britain, contained the subjoined provisions:

"Art. 2. The object of this league will be to carry into effect: (*a*), the evacuation of the country of Hanover and the north of Germany; (*b*), the establishment of the independence of the republics of Holland and Switzerland; (*c*), the reëstablishment of the King of Sardinia in Piedmont, with as large an augmentation of territory as circumstances will permit; (*d*), the future security of the kingdom of Naples, and the complete evacuation of Italy, the island of Elba included, by the French forces; (*e*), the establishment of an order of things in Europe which may effectually guarantee the security and independence of the different states, and present a solid barrier against future usurpations.

GRANVILLE LEVESON GOWER,
(Signed)   ADAM, PRINCE CZARTOCYSKI,
NICOLAS DE NOVOSSILZOFF."

Austria, Sweden and other northern powers ratified this treaty. Prussia and Naples remained neutral by special treaty with France. Napoleon I. organized his Grand Army, and crossed the Rhine, Sept. 26, 1805. He concluded an alliance with the Elector of Wurtemburg, who brought him a body of troops, called up Bavarian auxiliaries, made treaty with Baden, advanced into Prussia, Austria, and gained the great battle of Austerlitz, December 2, 1805, against the emperors of Austria and Prussia. The Peace of Presburg was then negotiated, depriving Austria of several provinces, of which Napoleon made gifts to Bavaria, Baden, and Wurtemburg, his German allies. By the Treaty of Presburg, both France and Austria resigned all claim of future sovereignty over Italy forever, by the following articles:

"III. His majesty the Emperor of Germany and Austria, for *himself, his heirs and successors*, recognizes the dispositions made by his majesty the Emperor of France, king of Italy, relative to the principalities of Lucca and Piombina. IV. His majesty the Emperor of Germany and Austria renounces, as well for himself, as for his *heirs and successors*, that part of the states of the Republic of Venice ceded to him by the treaties of Campo-Formio, and Luneville and they shall be united in perpetuity to the kingdom of Italy. V. His majesty the Emperor of Germany and Austria acknowledges his majesty the Emperor of France as king of Italy; *but it is agreed*, in conformity with the declaration made by his majesty the Emperor of the French at the moment when he took the crown of Italy, that as soon as the parties named in that declar-

ation shall have fulfilled the conditions therein expressed, the *crowns of Italy and France shall be separated forever* and *cannot in any case be united on the same head.* His majesty the Emperor of Germany binds himself to acknowledge, on the separation, the successor his majesty the Emperor of the French *shall appoint to himself as king of Italy.*"   (Signed)   CHAS. MONS. TALLEYRAND.
                                             JOHN, PRINCE OF LICHSTENSTEIN.
                                           IGUAZ, COUNT DE GYULAI.

The above mentioned declaration of Napoleon on taking the "crown of Italy," had occurred in his speech upon that occasion. "I shall keep this crown," he said to the Italians, "but only so long as your interests shall require; and I shall, with pleasure, see the moment arrive when I can place it on the head of a younger person, who, animated by my spirit, may continue my work and be on all occasions ready to sacrifice his person and interests to the security and happiness of the people over whom Providence, the constitutions of the kingdom, and my wish, shall have called him to reign." By the Treaty of Presburg, Austria resigned all she held of Italian territory, all of Venetian Istria and Dalmatia, and all forts and places in the Adriatic. A French memorial concerning the sequestration of Italy by Napoleon was issued about the same time, wherein the government declared its annexation policy to be in accordance with the wishes of the people of Parma, Piedmont, Piacenza, Genoa, and Venice, and concluded, curiously, with the remark that, "if it were allowed to compare trifles with objects of importance, it might be said, that *England had no right to complain* of the wish for a union between Liguria, (Genoa) and France, as France has made no complaint concerning the destruction of the Mahratta [East India] empire."

V.

Napoleon I. now began to dispose of his territorial acquisitions and tributary sovereignties, by dispensing liberal gifts to relatives and friends. He created General Murat Duke of Cleves and Berg, and made him his brother-in-law; gave his brother Joseph the kingdom of Naples and Sicily; bestowed Guastalla on his sister Pauline, and Neufchatel on Berthier, his war minister. He changed the Batavian Republic into a kingdom, for his brother Louis; made Talleyrand and Bernadotte dukes, and divided domains and lordships, in conquered countries, amongst his military followers. In July, 1806, he established the Confederacy of the Rhine, whereby Bavaria, Wurtemburg, Baden, Berg, Darmstadt, Nassau, Hohenzollern, and other German states became allies of France, and had their boundaries defined under imperial protection. One month later, Francis II. Emperor of Austria, resigned his office and title as Emperor of Germany, declaring the German empire to be abolished by the Rhenish Confederation, and falling back upon his hereditary rights as Emperor of the Austrian States. Prussia then declared war against France, but was invaded and conquered at the battle of Jena, in October, after which, Napoleon, at Berlin, organized a new government for Prussian territories, and issued his famous Berlin Decrees, declaring Great Britain in a state of blockade. Russia hastened to assist Prussia, but her power was broken at Eylau, in February, and a peace concluded between the emperors Napoleon, Alexander and Francis, at TILSIT, July 7th and 9th, 1807.

VI.

By this treaty Prussia lost a portion of her territory containing four millions of her subjects, including provinces on the Elbe, which Napoleon afterward erected into the Kingdom of Westphalia, for his brother Jerome. Russia and

Austria recognized Joseph Bonaparte to be King of Naples, and Louis Bonaparte to be King of Holland, and also acknowledged the Confederation of the Rhine. The Treaty of Tilsit was signed, respectively, by Talleyrand on the part of Napoleon, by Field-Marshal Kalkreuth and Count Augustus Goltz for Francis, and by Prince Alexander Kurakin and Prince Demetry Von Rostoff for Alexander. The intercourse of Napoleon and Alexander at Tilsit promoted a personal friendship between the two sovereigns. England grew apprehensive that secret articles of alliance had passed between them (*as, in our own day, there is said to be a secret understanding between the present Napoleon and Alexander.*) England also feared that Denmark would assist France with ships, and at once sent a fleet to bombard Copenhagen. Napoleon, in order to punish England, carried his diplomacy to Spain and Portugal. The Bourbons of Spain were at this period a disgrace to European thrones, the king being imbecile, and the queen an abandoned woman. Napoleon sent Marshal Junot to Portugal. On his approach, the Braganza family left their kingdom and fled to Brazil, their South-American vice-royalty. A convention was entered into between France and Manuel Godoy, the Spanish minister, whereby Spain was to be divided into several kingdoms. Meantime, the continental sovereigns began to make warlike preparations, and Napoleon brought about the CONGRESS OF ERFURT, with the view of concluding a general peace. This congress took place in September, 1808. Napoleon and Alexander met cordially, and the Austrian Emperor sent a polite note, excusing his absence, and assuring both his imperial cousins of his warmest friendship and esteem. A succession of feasts and conferences took place, and Napoleon succeeded in cementing his friendship with the Russian. The direct consequences of the meeting at Erfurt, were the withdrawal of French troops from Prussian towns, and an offer of peace by Russia and France to the British Government. Napoleon's desire was to gain time to subdue Spain, before England could stir up trouble in Germany. England, however, repelled negotiations, and sent her arms to the Spanish Peninsula. The Spanish war then broke out, and raged till Madrid was taken by the French, and Napoleon's brother, Joseph, proclaimed King of Spain. In Italy, during the same year, 1808, the crown of Naples was given to Murat, the Pope was deposed, and his states annexed to France. The Pope protested publicly, and was conducted, as a *quasi* prisoner, into French territory.

VII.

In 1809, Napoleon conceived it his policy to divorce his empress, Josephine, and ally himself to the House of Austria by a marriage with the Archduchess, Maria Louisa, daughter of the Emperor Francis. The marriage took place in March, 1810. Meantime, Louis, King of Holland, was deposed, as he had been crowned by his imperial brother, and the states of Holland and Hanse Towns, and part of Westphalia, were annexed to France. The Empire of Charlemagne was now reestablished, with nearly its ancient possessions, and three capitals, Paris, Rome, and Amsterdam. The Electorate of Hanover was joined to the Kingdom of Westphalia; the French conscription laws were extended over Naples on the south side, over Denmark on the north. An imperial decree was issued, restraining the press in all places under French control, by the establishment of a censorship. In August, 1807, the states of Sweden met to choose a king, and Marshal John Bernadotte, Prince of Monte Corvo, was elected under French influence. A great portion of all Europe was now under Napoleon's sway, though Spain continued to fight, and England refused peace or concessions. In the following year, 1811, a prince was born to the empire, and called King of Rome. About this period troubles arose between France and Russia ; and Sweden, under Bernadotte, began to murmur against French demands. Alexander of Russia had become less an admirer of Bonaparte, and was ready to take the position of his enemy. The consequences were soon apparent in a rupture, and Napoleon flattered himself with the hope of reducing all Russia under his power. Russia saw the impending storm, and prepared to meet it by an alliance with Great Britain, Sweden, and Spain, providing for defensive and offensive action against France.

VIII.

The war became general. Napoleon allied himself with Austria and Prussia, summoned his subordinate princes and states, and took the field for what he called a second Polish War. He had previously, in opposing Russia, made promises of restoring her nationality to Poland, which he failed to fulfill when he enjoyed the opportunity at Tilsit. The great campaign of 1812, began with gigantic resources—ended in bitter despair to its ambitious projector. Penetrating to Moscow, the Russians compelled his retreat by burning that ancient city ; and Bonaparte, pursued and harassed, led back to the Rhine a few shattered remnants of the Grand Army of Imperial France. His star began to set, and all Europe was prepared to revolt against him. The year 1812 closed upon reverses ; and the remainder of Napoleon's career, to his final fall, was a struggle against a succession of disasters. The German nationalities allied themselves with England and Russia. Foreign enemies increased continually, and even France abandoned the man to whom she owed everything. In April, 1814, Napoleon signed his first act of abdication at Paris, and was allowed by the victorious allies to retire to Elba. The Congress of Vienna was then convened, whilst the deposed sovereign watched its proceedings from his little island retreat. Then were negotiated the treaties of 1814–15, whose discussion was interrupted abruptly by Napoleon's return to France, and his renewed Empire of a Hundred Days.

IX.

By resolutions of the French Senate, April 3, 1814, under the presidency of Lavatar Count Barthelemy, the following decree had been adopted :
" ART. 1. Napoleon Bonaparte has forfeited the throne, and the hereditary right established in his family *is abolished.*
" ART. 2. The French people and the army are released from their oath of fidelity toward Napoleon Bonaparte."
On the 11th of April, Napoleon had signed the treaty of 1814 with the Allies, whereby he abdicated the French throne, and became an independent sovereign of the small island of Elba ; his empress, Maria Louisa, and her descendants, being allowed, as heritage, the Italian duchies of Parma, Piacenza, and Guastalla. On the 30th May following, the Treaty of Paris, between Louis XVIII. and the Allied Powers of Europe, was made. The articles of that treaty defined the boundaries of France, stripping her of all imperial acquisitions, and reducing her territory to the area that it embraced previous to the French Revolution :

"TREATY OF PEACE BETWEEN THE ALLIED POWERS AND FRANCE.

"In the name of the most Holy and undivided Trinity.

"His Majesty the King of France and Navarre, on the one part, and his Majesty the emperor of Austria, King of Hungary and Bohemia, and his Allies, on the other, being animated by an equal wish to put an end to the long agitations of Europe, and to the calamities of nations, by a solid peace, founded on a just distribution of force between the Powers, and containing in its stipulations the guaranty of its duration; and his Majesty the Emperor of Austria, King of Hungary and Bohemia, and his Allies, no longer wishing to exact, from France, at the present moment, when being replaced under the paternal government of her kings, she thus offers to Europe a pledge of security and stability, conditions and guaranties which they had to demand with regret under her late government; their said Majesties have appointed Plenipotentiaries to discuss, conclude, and sign a treaty of peace and friendship; that is to say—

"Art. II. The kingdom of France preserves the integrity of its limits such as they existed at the period of the 1st of January, 1792. It shall receive beside, augmentation of territory comprised within the line of demarkation fixed by the following article :

"Art. III. On the side of Belgium, Germany, and Italy, the ancient frontier, such as it existed on the 1st January, 1792, shall be reëstablished, the same commencing from the North Sea, between Dunkirk and Newport, even unto the Mediterranean between Cagnes and Nice, with the following rectifications :

"1. In the department of Jemappes, the cantons of Dour, Morbes-le-château, Beaumont, and Chimay, shall remain to France ; the line of demarkation, where it touches the canton of Dour, shall pass between that canton and those of Boussu and Paturage, as well as, further on, between that of Morbes-le-Château, and those of Biuch and Thuin.

"2. In the department of the Sambre and Meuse, the cantons of Valcourt, Florennes, Beauraing, and Godume, shall belong to France ; the demarkation, upon reaching this department, shall follow the line which separates the fore-mentioned cantons, from the department of Jemappes, and from the rest of that of the Sambre and Meuse.

"3. In the department of the Moselle, the new demarkation, where it differs from the old, shall be formed by a line to be drawn from Perle as far as Fremersdsdorf, or by that which separates the canton of Tholey from the rest of the department of the Moselle.

"4. In the department of the Sarre, the cantons of Saarbruck and Arnwal, shall remain to France, as well as that part of the canton of Lebach, which is situated to the south of a line to be drawn along the confines of the villages of Herchenbach, Ueberhosen, Hilsbach, and Hall (leaving these different places without the French frontier) to the point where, taken from Querselle (which belongs to France), the line which separates the cantons of Arnwal and Ottweiler, reaches that which separates those of Arnwal and Lebach ; the frontier on this side shall be formed by the line above marked out, and, then by that which separates the canton of Arnwal from that of Bliescastel.

"5. The fortress of Landau having, prior to the year 1792, formed an insulated point in Germany, France retains beyond her frontiers a part of the departments of Mont Tonnerre and the Lower Rhine in order to join the fortress of Landau and its district to the rest of the kingdom.' The new demarkation, proceeding from the point where, at Obersteinbach (which remains without the French frontier), the frontier enters the department of the Moselle, and that of Mont Tonnerre, joins the department of the Lower Rhine, shall follow the line which separates the cantons of Wissenburgh and Bergzabern (on the side of France) from the cantons of Pirmasens, Dahn, and Anweiler (on the side of Germany), to the point where these limits, near the village of Wohnersheim, touch the ancient district of the fortress of Landau. Of this district, which remains as it was in 1792, the new frontier shall follow the arm of the river Queich, which in leaving this district near Queichheim (which rests with France), passes near the villages of Merlenheim, Kniltelsheim, and Belheim (also remaining French), to the Rhine, which thence continues the boundary between France and Germany. As to the Rhine, the Thalweg, or course of the river, shall form the boundary ; the changes, however, which may occur in the course of the river, shall have no effect on the property of the isles which are found there. The possession of these isles shall be replaced under the same form as at the period of the treaty of Luneville.

"6. In the department of the Doubs, the frontier shall be drawn, so as to commence above La Ranconnière near the Loell, and follow the crest of the Jura between Cerneaux Pequignot and the village of Fontenelles, so far as that summit of the Jura which lies about seven or eight miles to the northwest of the village of La Brevine, where it will turn back within the ancient limits of France.

"7. In the department of the Leman, the frontiers between the French territory, the Pais de Vaud, and the different portions of the territory of Geneva, (which shall make a part of Switzerland), remain as they were before the incorporation of Geneva with France. But the canton of Frangy, that of St. Julien (with exception of that part lying to the north of a line to be drawn from the point where the river of La Laire enters near Chancey into the Genevese territory, along the borders of Seseguin, Laconex, and Seseneuve, which shall remain without the limits of France), the canton of Regnier (with exception of that portion which lies eastward of a line following the borders of the Muraz, Bussy, Pers, and Cornier, which shall be without the French limits), and the canton of La Roche (with exception of the places named La Roche and Armanay with their districts) shall rest with France. The frontier shall follow the limits of those different cantons and the lines separating those portions which France retains from those she gives up.

"8. In the department of Mont Blanc, France shall obtain the Suprefecture of Chambery, (with exceptions of the cantons de l'Hôpital, St. Pierre d'Albigny, La Rocette and Montmelian,) the Suprefecture of Annecy, (with exception of that part of the canton of Faverges, situated to the east of a line passing between Ourechaise and Marlens on the French side, and Marthod and Ugine on the opposite side, and which then follows the crest of the mountains to the frontier of the canton of Thones). This line, with the limits of the afore-named cantons, shall constitute the new frontier on this side.

"On the side of the Pyrenees, the frontiers remain as they were, between the two kingdoms of France and Spain, on the 1st of January, 1792. There shall be appointed on the part of both, a mutual commission, to arrange their final demarkation.

"France renounces all claims of sovereignty, supremacy, and possession over all countries, districts, towns, and places whatsoever, situated without the above stated frontier. The principality of Monaco is replaced in the same situation as on the 1st of January, 1792.

"The Allied Courts assure to France the possession of the principality of Avignon, the Venaisin, the county of Montbeliard, and all the inclosed districts once belonging to Germany, comprised within the above indicated frontier, which had been incorporated with France before or after the 1st of January, 1792.

"The Powers preserve mutually the full right to fortify whatever point of their states they may judge fitting for their safety.

"To avoid all injury to private property, and to protect on the most liberal principles the possessions of individuals domiciliated on the frontiers, there shall be named by each of the States adjoining to France, Commissioners, to proceed jointly with French Commissioners, to the demarkation of their respective boundaries. So soon as the office of these Commissioners shall be completed, instruments shall be drawn up, signed by them, and posts erected to mark the mutual limits.

"Art. IV. To secure the communications of the town of Geneva with the other parts of the Swiss territory on the Lake, France consents, that the road by Versoy shall be common to the two countries. The respective Governments will have an amicable understanding on the means of preventing smuggling, the regulation of the posts, and the maintenance of the road.

"Art. V. The navigation of the Rhine, from the point where it becomes navigable to the sea, and back, shall be free, so as to be interdicted to no person. Principles shall be laid down at a future Congress, for the collection of the duties by the States on the banks, in the manner most equal and favorable to the commerce of all nations.

"It shall be also inquired and ascertained at the same Congress, in what mode, for the purposes of more facile communication and rendering nations continually less strangers to each other, this disposition may be extended to all rivers that in their navigable course separate or traverse different States.

"Art. VI. Holland, placed under the sovereignty of the House of Orange, shall receive an increase of territory. The title, and the exercise of its sovereignty, cannot, under any circumstances, belong to a prince wearing or designated to wear a foreign crown.

"The German States shall be independent, and united by a federative league.

"Independent Switzerland shall continue under its own Government. Italy, without the limits of the countries which shall return to Austria, shall be composed of Sovereign States.

"Art. VII. The Island of Malta and its dependencies shall belong, in full possession and sovereignty, to his Britannic Majesty."

X.

The Congress of Vienna met, pursuant to provision of the Treaty of Paris, but its deliberations were interrupted by the landing of Napoleon once more upon French soil, where he was welcomed by a revolt of the army. The returned general assumed his imperial title, and issued a proclamation to the French people, March 1st, 1815, which was answered by a declaration of the Allied Powers at Vienna, on the 13th of the same month, as follows :

"DECLARATION.

"The Powers who have signed the treaty of Paris, assembled in Congress at Vienna, being informed of the escape of Napoleon Bonaparte, and of his entrance into France with an armed force, owe it to their dignity and the interest of social order, to make a solemn declaration of the sentiments which this event has excited in them.

"By thus breaking the convention which established him in the Island of Elba, Bonaparte destroys the only legal title on which his existence depended: by appearing again in France with projects of confusion and disorder, he has deprived himself of the protection of the law, and has manifested to the Universe, that there can be neither peace nor truce with him. The powers consequently declare, that Napoleon Bonaparte has placed himself without the pale of civil and social relations, and that as an enemy and disturber of the tranquillity of the world, he has rendered himself liable to public vengeance.

"They declare, at the same time, that, firmly resolved to maintain entire the treaty of Paris, of 30th of May, 1814, and the dispositions sanctioned by that treaty, and those which they have resolved on, or shall hereafter resolve on, to complete and to consolidate it, they will employ all their means, and will unite all their efforts, that the general peace, the object of the wishes of Europe, and the constant purpose of their labors, may not again be troubled, and to guarantee against every attempt which shall threaten to replunge the world into the disorders and miseries of revolutions.

"And although entirely persuaded that all France, rallying round its legitimate sovereign, will immediately annihilate this attempt of a criminal and impotent delirium ; all the sovereigns of Europe, animated by the same sentiments, and guided by the same principles, declare, that if, contrary to all calculations, there should result from this event any real danger, they will be ready to give the King of France and to the French nation, or to any other government that shall be attacked, so soon as they shall be called upon, all the assistance requisite to restore public tranquillity; and to make a common cause against all those who should undertake to compromise it.

"The present declaration inserted in the Register of the Congress assembled at Vienna on the 18th of March, 1815, shall be made public.

"Done and attested by the Plenipotentiaries of the High Powers who signed the Treaty of Paris.

"VIENNA, March 13, 1815.

"Here follow the signatures in the alphabetical order of the Courts :

Austria.	Prince METTERNICH,
	Baron WESSENBERG.
Spain.	P. GOMEZ LABRADOR.
France.	Prince TALLEYRAND,
	Duke of DALBERG,
	LATOUR DU PIN,
	Count ALEXIS DU NOAILLES.
Gt. Brit.	WELLINGTON,
	CLANCARTY,
	CATHCART,
	STEWART.
Portugal.	Count PALMELA SALDANHA LOBC.
Prussia.	Prince HARDENBERG,
	Baron HUMBOLDT.
Russia.	Count RASUMOWSKY,
	Count STACKELBERG.
	Count NESSELRODE.
Sweden.	LOEWENHELM."

XI.

The Hundred Days, during which Napoleon made head against the Allies, ended by his second abdication. Previous to the battle of Waterloo, he entered into secret negotiation with the Congress of Vienna, with a view to conclude a peace on the basis of the Treaty of Paris. His designs were baffled by the indignation excited on account of an expedition which Murat, deposed King of Naples, undertook in April. On the 22d June, 1815, Napoleon finally resigned his crown, though still declaring his son emperor, and naming a Regency. The armies of the Allies then overran France, and on the 20th November, 1815, the second Treaty of Paris was made, as follows:

" DEFINITIVE TREATY

" In the name of the Most Holy and Undivided Trinity,

" Article 1. The frontiers of France shall be the same as they were in the year 1790, save and except the modifications on one side and on the other, which are detailed in the present Article. First, on the northern frontiers, the line of demarkation shall remain as it was fixed by the Treaty of Paris, as far as opposite to Quiverain, from thence it shall follow the ancient limits of the Belgian Provinces, of the late Bishopric of Liege, and of the Duchy of Bouillon, as they existed in the year 1790, leaving the territories included within that line, of Philippeville and Marienbourg, with the fortresses so-called, together with the whole of the Duchy of Bouillon, without the frontiers of France. From Villers near Orval upon the confines of the Department Des Ardennes, and of the Grand Duchy of Luxembourg as far as Perle, upon the great road leading from Thionville to Treves, the line shall remain as it was laid down by the Treaty of Paris. From Perle it shall pass by Launsdorff, Walwich, Schardorff, Niederveiling, Pelweiler (all these places with their *Banlieues* or dependencies remaining to France), to Houvre; and shall follow from thence the old limits of the district of Sarrebruck, leaving Saarelouis, and the course of the Sarre, together with the places situated to the right of the line above described, and their *Banlieues* or dependencies, without the limits of France. From the limits of the district of Sarrebruck the line of demarkation shall be the same, which at present separates from Germany the departments of the Moselle and of the Lower Rhine, as far as to the Lauter, which river shall from thence serve as the Frontier until it shall fall into the Rhine. All the territory on the left bank of the Lauter, including the fortress of Landau, shall form part of Germany.

" The town of Weissenbourg, however, through which that river runs, shall remain entirely to France, with a *rayon* on the left bank, not exceeding a thousand toises, and which shall be more particularly determined by the Commissioners who shall be charged with the approaching designation of the boundaries. Secondly, leaving the mouth of the Lauter, and continuing along the departments of the Lower Rhine, the Upper Rhine, the Doubs, and the Jura, to the Canton de Vaud, the frontiers shall remain as fixed by the Treaty of Paris. The Thalweg of the Rhine shall form the boundary between France and the States of Germany, but the property of the islands shall remain in perpetuity, as it shall be fixed by a new survey of the course of that river, and continue unchanged, whatever variation that course may undergo in the lapse of time. Commissioners shall be named on both sides, by the High Contracting Parties, within the space of three months, to proceed upon the said survey. One half of the bridge between Strasbourg and Kehl shall belong to France, and the other half to the Grand Duchy of Baden. Thirdly, in order to establish a direct communication between the Canton of Geneva and Switzerland, that part of the Pays de Gex, bounded on the east by the lake Leman; on the south, by the territory of the Canton of Geneva; on the north by that of the Canton de Vaud; on the west, by the course of the Versoix, and by a line which comprehends the communes of Collex Bossy, and Meyrin, leaving the commune of Ferney to France, shall be ceded to the Helvetic Confederacy, in order to be united to the Canton of Geneva. The line of the French custom-houses shall be placed to the west of the Jura, so that the whole of the Pays de Gex shall be without that line. Fourthly, from the frontiers of the Canton of Geneva, as far as the Mediterranean, the line of demarkation shall be that which, in the year 1790, separated France from Savoy, and from the county of Nice. The relations which the Treaty of Paris of 1814 had reëstablished between France and the Principality of Monaco, shall cease forever, and the same relations shall exist between that Principality and his Majesty the King of Sardinia. Fifthly, all the territories and districts included within the boundary of the French territory, as determined by the present Articles, shall remain united to France. Sixthly, the High Contracting Parties shall name, within three months after the signature of the present Treaty, Commissioners to regulate every thing relating to the designation of the boundaries of the respective countries, and as soon as the labors of the Commissioners shall have terminated, maps shall be drawn, and landmarks shall be erected, which shall point out the respective limits.

" 8. All the dispositions of the Treaty of Paris of the 30th of May, 1814, relative to the countries ceded by that treaty, shall equally apply to the several territories and districts ceded by the present treaty.

" In witness whereof, the respective Plenipotentiaries have signed the same, and have affixed thereunto the seals of their arms.

" Done at Paris this 20th day of November, in the year of our Lord, 1815.

(Signed)

[L. S.]	CASTLEREAGH.
[L. S.]	WELLINGTON.
[L. S.]	RICHELIEU."

XII.

On the 19th April, 1815, Francis I. of Austria, issued his proclamation concerning the Lombardo-Venetian Kingdom, as follows:

"PROCLAMATION OF THE EMPEROR OF AUSTRIA.

" VIENNA, *April* 14.

" We, Francis the First, by the Grace of God Emperor of Austria, King of Hungary, Bohemia, Lombardy, and Venice, Galicia and Lodomiria, etc. etc., Archduke of Austria.

" In consequence of the treaties concluded with the Allied Powers, and further Conventions concluded with them, the Provinces of Lombardy and Venice, in their whole extent, as far as Lago Maggiore, the river Ticino, and the Po, together with part of the territory of Mantua on the right bank of the latter river, also the province of the Valtelin, the counties of Chiavenna and Bormio, are incorporated with the Austrian imperial dominions, and united to them forever as an integral part.

" Animated with the most ardent desire to confer on the inhabitants of these provinces and districts an unequivocal proof of our imperial affection, and the high value we set upon this union, and also to give them an additional guaranty for the close ties which henceforth bind them to us, we have thought fit to create the above-mentioned provinces and districts into a kingdom, by the title of the kingdom of Lombardy and Venice, and have, therefore, published these presents for the purpose of making known to every one this our Imperial determination.

" [Here follow the Articles, fifteen in number. Among other provisions it appears, that the Iron Crown and the Order with that Title were to be retained, that the kingdom was to be governed by a Viceroy, and divided into two Governments, of which Milan and Venice should be the capitals.]"

XIII.

The treaty which Great Britain concluded with Sardinia, May 15th, 1815, defined the limits of Sardinian territory as follows :

" TREATY BETWEEN GREAT BRITAIN AND SARDINIA, SIGNED AT VIENNA, THE 20TH MAY, 1815.

" His Majesty the King of Sardinia, etc., etc., being restored to the full and entire possession of his Continental States, in the same manner as he possessed them on the 1st of January, 1792, and to the whole of them, with the exception of the part of Savoy ceded to France by the treaty of Paris of the 30th May, 1814; certain changes having since been agreed upon, during the Congress of Vienna, relative to the extent and limits of the said states.

" Plenipotentiaries—The Earl of Clancarty, etc. : the Sieurs Don Anthony Maria Philip Asinari, Marquis de St. Marsan, etc. ; and Count Don Joachim Alexander Rossi, etc.

" Art. 1. The frontiers of the states of his majesty the King of Sardinia shall be, on the side of France, such as they were on the 1st of January, 1792, with the exception of the changes effected by the treaty of Paris of the 30th May, 1814.

" On the side of the Helvetic Confederation, such as they existed on the 1st of January, 1792, with the exception of the change produced by the cession, in favor of the Canton of Geneva, as specified in the 7th article hereinafter inserted.

" On the side of the states of his majesty the Emperor of Austria, such as they existed on the 1st of January, 1792; and the Convention concluded between their majesties the Empress Maria Theresa and the King of Sardinia, on the 4th of October, 1751, shall be reciprocally confirmed in all its stipulations.

" On the side of the states of Parma and Placentia, the frontier, as far as it concerns the ancient states of the king of Sardinia, shall continue to be the same as it was on the 1st of January, 1792.

" The borders of the former states of Genoa, and of the countries called Imperial Fiefs, united to the States of his majesty the King of Sardinia, according to the following articles, shall be the same as those which, on the 1st of January, 1792, separated those countries from the states of Parma and Placentia, and from those of Tuscany and Massa.

" The island of Capraja having belonged to the ancient Republic of Genoa, is included in the cession of the States of Genoa to his majesty the King of Sardinia.

" Art. 2. The states which constituted the former Republic of Genoa. are united in perpetuity to those of his majesty the King of Sardinia; to be, like the latter, possessed by him in full sovereignty and hereditary property, and to descend, in the male line, in the order of primogeniture, to the two branches of this house, viz., the royal branch and the branch of Savoy Carignan.

" Art. 3. The King of Sardinia shall add to his present titles that of Duke of Genoa.

" Art. 5. The countries called Imperial Fiefs, formerly united to the ancient Ligurian Republic, are definitively united to the states of his majesty the King of Sardinia, in the same manner as the rest of the Genoese States ; and the inhabitants of these countries shall enjoy the same rights and privileges as those of the states of Genoa, specified in the preceding article.

" Art. 6. The right that the powers who signed the treaty of Paris of the 30th May, 1814, reserved to themselves, by the 3d article of that treaty, of fortifying such points of their states as they might judge proper for their safety, is equally reserved, without restriction, to his majesty the King of Sardinia.

" Art. 7. His majesty the King of Sardinia cedes to the canton of Geneva, the district of Savoy specified in the article, intituled ' B. B. Cession made by his majesty the King of Sardina to the canton of Geneva,' and on the conditions specified in the same act.

" Art. 8. The provinces of Chablais and Faucigny and the whole of the territory of Savoy to the north of Ugine, belonging to his majesty the King of Sardinia, shall form a part of the neutrality of Switzerland, as recognized and guaranteed by all the powers.

" Wherever, therefore, the neighboring powers to Switzerland are in a state of open or impending hostility, the troops of his majesty the King of Sardinia, which may be in those provinces, shall retire, and may for that purpose pass through the Vallais, if necessary. No other armed troops of any other power shall have the privilege of passing through, or remaining in the said territories and provinces, excepting those which the Swiss Confederation shall think proper to place there; it being well understood that this state of things shall not in any manner interrupt the administration of these countries, in which the civil agents of his majesty the King of Sardinia may likewise employ the municipal guard for the preservation of good order.

"Art. 9. The present treaty shall foi m part of the definitive arrangements of the Congress of Vienna.

"Done at Vienna, the 20th of May, in the year of our Lord 1815.

"Signed,

[L. S.]	The Prince de METTERNICH.
[L. S.]	The Marquis de St. MARSAN.
[L. S.]	The Baron de WESSENBURG.
[L. S.]	The Count ROSSI."

XIV.

The following treaty, entered into by Austria, Prussia, and Russia, Sept. 26, 1815, and subsequently approved by the British government, forms the substance of that agreement between the principal allies, which has since been known as the Holy Alliance, on account of the solemn religious professions made by the high contracting parties :

"HOLY ALLIANCE TREATY, SEPT. 26, 1815.

"In the name of the Most Holy and Indivisible Trinity.

"Their majesties the Emperor of Austria, the King of Prussia, and the Emperor of Russia, having, in consequence of the great events which have marked the course of the three last years in Europe, and especially of the blessings which it has pleased Divine Providence to shower down upon those states, which place their confidence and their hope on it alone, acquired the intimate conviction of the necessity of founding the conduct to be observed by the powers in their reciprocal relations upon the sublime truths which the holy religion of our Saviour teaches—

"They solemnly declare that the present act has no other object than to publish in the face of the whole world, their fixed resolution, both in the administration of their respective states, and their political relations with every other government, to take for their sole guide the precepts of that holy religion ; namely, the precepts of justice, Christian charity, and peace, which, far from being applicable only to private concerns, must have an immediate influence on the councils of princes, and guide all their steps, as being the only means of consolidating human institutions, and remedying their imperfections. In consequence their majesties have agreed on the following articles :

"Art. 1. Conformably to the words of the holy Scriptures, which command all men to consider each other as brethren, the three contracting monarchs will remain united by the bonds of a true and indissoluble fraternity, and considering each other as fellow countrymen, they will on all occasions, and in all places, lend each other aid and assistance; and regarding themselves toward their subjects and armies as fathers of families, they will lead them, in the same spirit of fraternity with which they are animated, to project religion, peace, and justice.

Art. 2. In consequence, the sole principle in force, whether between the said governments or between their subjects, shall be that of doing each other reciprocal service, and of testifying by unalterable good will, the mutual affection with which they ought to be animated, to consider themselves all as members of one and the same Christian nation, the three allied princes looking on themselves as merely delegated by providence to govern three branches of the one family, namely, Austria, Prussia, and Russia; thus confessing that the Christian world, of which they and their people form a part, has, in reality, no other sovereign than him to whom alone power really belongs, because in him alone are found all the treasures of love, science, and infinite wisdom, that is to say, God, our divine Saviour, the Word of the Most High, the Word of Life. Their majesties consequently recommend to their people, with the most tender solicitude, as the sole means of enjoying that peace which arises from a good conscience, and which alone is durable, to strengthen themselves every day more and more in the principles and exercise of the duties which the divine Saviour has taught to mankind.

"Art. 3. All the powers who shall choose solemnly to avow the sacred principles which have dictated the present act, and shall acknowledge how important it is for the happiness of nations, too long agitated, that these truths should henceforth exercise over the destinies of mankind all the influence which belongs to them, will be received with equal ardor and affection into this holy alliance.

"Done in triplicate, and signed at Paris, the year of grace, 1815, 14th (26th) September.

[L. S.]	FRANCIS.
[L. S.]	FREDERICK WILLIAM.
[L. S.]	ALEXANDER.

At a later period the governments concerned in this holy alliance, entered into a secret treaty, defining motives and ulterior objects involved. This secret treaty occupies its due place in our retrospect, and furnishes a key to subsequent political changes in Italian, Hungarian, and Bohemian administration under Austrian influence. A dynastic opposition to liberalism in all forms has been the covert understanding between Austria, Prussia, and Russia, from the signing of the Holy Alliance treaty, in 1815, throughout all encroachments and usurpations of those powers, up to the present war of Italian nationality.

3

XV.

The restoration of Austria's territory to the extent that she claimed before Napoleon Bonaparte expelled her governors from Italy, was agreed upon with Russia, Prussia, and Great Britain, by a secret article of the Treaty of Toepletz, made between the Allies in 1815.   Consequently, the Congress of Vienna gave back to Francis I. all the Italian provinces he had ceded to Napoleon by the Treaty of Campo Formio, in 1797 ; by that of Luneville, in 1801 ; Presburg, in 1805 ; Fontainebleau, in 1807 ; and Vienna, in 1809.   These retrocessions embraced Venice, and all territory between the Ticino, the Po, and the Adriatic, that now constitute the Lombardo-Venetian Kingdom ; together with the valleys of the Vattelene, Bormio, and Chiavenna.   Belgium and former Austrian possessions in Suabia were not restored. . . . . . The duchy of MODENA was assigned to Archduke Francis of Este, connected by marriage with the House of Austria ; and .the duchy of MASSA and CARARA was given to Archduchess Maria Beatrix of Este ; both duchies being reversible to the House of Austria. . . . . The grand-duchy of TUSCANY was restored to Archduke Ferdinand of Austria, and augmented by other territory. . . . . . The duchy of LUCCA was vested in the Infanta Maria Louisa of Spain, and made reversible to the grand-duchy of Tuscany. . . . . . The Two Sicilies went back to Ferdinand IV. . . . . . . PIEDMONT, SAVOY, and the states of the former Genoese Republic, were restored to the King of Sardinia.

XVI.

The French government continued under Louis XVIII. till 1824, when he died, and his brother, Charles X., succeeded.   An aristocratic spirit was encouraged, and the government sought to revive the ancient dominion of king and church.   In 1825, on the occasion of Lafayette's return to France, after his last visit to the United States, a demonstration of welcome was made by citizens of Havre, which was suppressed by military force.   Jesuits began to gain control of the courts and bureaux, and so many were the assumptions of the government that a strong liberal party arose to oppose its encroachments. A rigorous censorship of the press was one of the results.   In the beginning of 1830, an army of 40,000 was sent to subdue Algiers, and thus the nucleus of the present African Army was established.   About this time, the three governments of France, Russia, and Great Britain united to settle the affairs of Greece, and erect that struggling commonwealth into a kingdom.   In July, 1830, a popular revolution broke out in Paris, and in three days the Bourbon dynasty was overthrown, and Louis Philippe, Duke of Orleans, was made Lieutenant-General of the Kingdom.   On the 9th August, Louis Philippe was chosen king by the Chamber of Deputies, and subscribed to all liberal changes that were demanded.

XVII.

Louis Philippe, " King of the French," occupied his throne during eighteen years.   The immediate causes of his overthrow, and the Revolution of 1848, were over-taxation suffered by the people, and corrupt administration of the public finances.   The king's minister, M. Guizot, became unpopular, and a strong republican party was formed, headed by M. Thiers and M. Odillon Barrat.   A series of Reform Banquets (so called) were held, which, like the " clubs" of 1789, were the nuclei of disaffection toward government.   These banquets were suppressed through government interference, but the spirit of revolution had been aroused ; and, February 23, 1848, barricades were thrown up in the streets of Paris. The National Guard was called out by the ministry, but they joined the people, and toward evening fighting commenced. The king, becoming alarmed, summoned Thiers and Barrot, to form a liberal ministry, and issued a proclamation promising reform ; but these measures were adopted too late. Next morning, M. Emile Girardin, editor of *La Presse*, a Paris journal, who was a member of the Chamber of Deputies, appeared before the king, and demanded his abdication. After some hesitation, Louis Philippe signed a paper, resigning authority to the Count of Paris, his grandson. His daughter-in-law, widow of the Duc d'Orleans, presented her son to the deputies, as their king, but they refused to receive him. *"Il'est trop tard!"* "It is too late!" was their response ; and this decision banished the House of Orleans from France. Louis Philippe immediately fled, with his family, and took refuge in England, while a provisional government was constituted, composed of Dupont de l'Eure, Lamartine, Ledru Rollin, Arago, Garnier Pages, Marie, and Cremieux. The republic was immediately proclaimed, a revolutionary army enrolled, under the name of the Garde Mobile, and preparations made to establish a permanent government. The Parisian multitude, mainly consisting of workmen and others thrown out of employment, with ten or fifteen thousand democratic refugees from other countries and the interior, demanded a republican war, as in 1790 ; whilst the Provisional Government, influenced by Lamartine, issued daily decrees, in eloquent language, proclaiming universal peace, the repeal of laws inflicting death punishments, and the abolition of slavery in all French colonies. Meantime, the army pronounced in favor of the republic, and to sustain the bankrupt government an issue of paper money was made on security of the national lands. Great social distress, however, arose from the stoppage of manufactures and withdrawal of capital from trade. To remedy this, the government established national workshops, and to these an army of 120,000 destitute men repaired each Monday morning to find employment for scarcely half their numbers, and on Saturday night to draw a week's stipend from government for useless labor. The vast forces of unemployed men were neither vagabonds nor ruffians, but persons in absolute necessity, and anxious to be occupied. Lamartine alluded to them, at a later day, as follows : " To workmen of the hand were soon joined laborers in the liberal arts, who had also exhausted their last resources ; artists, designers, compositors, employees of the book-trade, clerks, men of letters, actors, men who had only handled the graver, the press, or the pen, came courageously to demand at the workshops a pickaxe or mattock, to dig ground in the *Champ de Mars*, or to labor in the different timber-yards to which they were assigned. They met at morning in the boulevards, in the *Champs Elysées*, in all quarters of the faubourgs, in small detachments of from twenty to a hundred men, of all ages and costumes, marching, preceded by a banner, and conducted to labor by a brigadier. These men were sad in countenance, but at first serious and patient." During the experiment of the workshops, a new National Assembly was elected by universal suffrage, and this body endeavored to organize a permanent republican government ; but a popular demonstration in Paris was followed by the military dictatorship of General Cavaignac, and subsequently by the election of Louis Napoleon Bonaparte as President of the Republic. The events that followed, in France, comprising Louis Napoleon's *coup d'état*, by which he dissolved the Chamber of Deputies, and his reëlection for ten years as President, with his final assumption of imperial title and power, are familiar to all.

XVIII.

In order to possess ourselves of a correct understanding regarding events which, during a dozen years back, have agitated Europe to greater or less commotion, we may revert briefly to the Rhenish Confederation established under Napoleon's protection in 1806, remarking that this organization gave place to the present Germanic Confederation, and follow the central European states through some phases of their history since 1815. The Confederation of the Rhine was dismembered by the general alliance against Bonaparte in 1814, and the Germanic Confederation was agreed upon by the following articles:

"GERMAN ACT OF CONFEDERATION.

"Art. 1. The Sovereign Princes and free cities of Germany, including their Majesties the Emperor of Austria and the Kings of Prussia, Denmark, and the Netherlands, namely, the Emperor of Austria and the King of Prussia, for those of their possessions which formerly belonged to the German Empire, the King of Denmark for Holstein, the King of the Netherlands for the Grand Duchy of Luxemburg, unite themselves into a perpetual league, which shall be called the German Confederation.

"2. The object thereof is the maintenance of the internal and external security of Germany, and of the independence and inviolability of the different German States.

"3. The Members of the Confederation have, as such, equal rights; they bind themselves, all equally to maintain the act of Confederation.

"4. The affairs of the Confederation shall be managed by a general assembly, in which all the Members of the Confederation shall be represented by their plenipotentiaries, who shall each have one vote either severally, or as representing more than one member, as follows:

"Austria 1 vote, Prussia 1, Bavaria 1, Saxony 1, Hanover 1, Wurtemberg 1, Baden 1, Electorate of Hesse 1, Grand Duchy of Hesse 1, Denmark for Holstein 1, the Netherlands for Luxemburg 1, the Grand-Ducal and Ducal Saxon Houses 1, Brunswick and Nassau 1, Mecklenburg Schwerin, and Mecklenburg Strelitz 1. Holstein Oldenburg, Anhalt, and Schwartzburg 1, Hohenzollern, Lichtenstein, Reuss, Schaumberg Lippe, Lippe and Waldeck 1, the free cities of Lubeck, Frankfort, Bremen, and Hamburgh 1; total 17 votes.

"5. Austria has the presidency in the Diet of the Confederation; every member of the league is empowered to make propositions and bring them under discussion; and the presiding member is bound to submit such propositions for deliberation within a fixed period.

"6. When these propositions relate to the abolition or alteration of the fundamental laws of the Confederation, or to regulations relating to the Act of Confederation itself, then the Diet forms itself into a full committee, when the different component members shall have the following votes proportioned to the extent of their territories:

"Austria, Prussia, Saxony, Bavaria, Hanover, and Wurtemburg, four votes each; Baden, Electorate of Hesse, Grand Duchy of Hesse, Holstein, and Luxemburg, three votes each; Brunswick, Mecklenburg-Schwerin, and Nassau, two votes each; Saxe Weimar, and a great number of minor German Princes, with the free towns, one vote each; total 69 votes.

"7. Questions in the Diet shall be decided by a simple majority of votes, on ordinary occasions, the President to have the casting vote; but when in full committee, the question must be decided by a majority of at least three-fourths.

"8. The Diet of the Confederation has its sitting at Frankfort-on-the-Main; its opening is fixed for the 1st of September, 1815.

"9. The first business of the Diet, after its opening, will be the formation of the organic regulations of the Confederation, in regard to its external, military, and internal relations.

"10. Every Member of the Confederation engages to assist in protecting not only all Germany, but every separate State of the league against any attack, and reciprocally to guarantee to each other the whole of their possessions included within the Confederation.

"After war has been once declared by the Confederation, no member can enter into separate negotiations with the enemy, nor conclude a separate armistice or peace.

"Although the members possess the right of alliance of every kind, yet they bind themselves to enter into no treaties hostile to the security of the Confederation, or to that of any Confederate State.

"The Members of the League also bind themselves not to make war on each other under any pretext, nor to decide their differences by force, but to bring them under the consideration and decision of the Diet."

XIX.

The treaties of Vienna, in "settling the peace of Europe," defined the bounds of German confederated States. Their "settlement" was based on a dynastic balance of power, from which, of course, the more powerful governments reaped superior advantages. The dynastic adjustment was guided by traditions of "legitimacy" (so called) which claimed certain hereditary rights to territory and sovereignty for certain reigning families. But it is known to historical students that no real ancestral foundation is to be traced for any of the assumptions of German or Italian princes. The "legitimate" ancient mode of conferring sovereign power, in both Germany and Italy, was through election of rulers, either by people at large, or classes of communities. From generation to generation, through scores of centuries, the chiefs of those two countries were allowed their authority only by voice of constituent assemblies. Even in the holy Roman or German Empire, of which Austrian dominion is a continuation, the monarchs were all created by the suffrages of independent minor chieftains. Albert of Hapsburg, the first Austrian emperor of Germany, was thus elevated to his dignity, and the hereditary succession was only established by military conquest and the law of force. In a similar manner, the Pope of Rome has always been elected by votes of the College of Cardinals ; and all the dukedoms, principalities, and other sovereignties of Italy were preceded by and founded upon republican states, whereof government was usurped through success in arms or diplomacy. The kings of Poland, of Sweden, of Holland, of France, of Saxony ; the chiefs of Malta, of Rhodes, of the Grecian Isles, were elective during the middle ages, as well as at periods before. Either from *elected* sovereigns or usurpers all the "legitimacy" of present dynasties must trace descent. Hence, though the French Revolution overturned thrones, and dismembered territories, it invaded no actual *legitimate* rights of regal succession, because such rights had no real foundation. When, therefore, by the settlement of Europe, its map was revised, and governments reconstructed, the allied powers sought only to balance their power, by getting each as much sovereignty and possession as it could claim from the weakness or ignorance of the rest. Such was the result of the famous treaties of Vienna, which re-divided and portioned Europe according to the agreement of a dozen plenipotentiaries.

XX.

The Germanic Confederation consisted of thirty-eight states, as follows : 1, Austria (by virtue of her German States) ; 2, Prussia ; 3, Bavaria ; 4, Saxony ; 5, Hanover ; 6, Wurtemburg ; 7, Baden ; 8, Hesse-Cassel ; 9, Hesse-Darmstadt ; 10, Denmark (which casts a vote through her German provinces, Holstein and Lauenburg) ; 11, The Netherlands (which appears through her possession of Luxemburg) ; 12, Mecklenburg-Schwerin ; 13, Nassau ; 14, Saxe-Weimar ; 15, Saxe-Coburg-Gotha ; 16, Saxe-Meiningen ; 17, Saxe-Altenburg ; 18, Brunswick ; 19, Mecklenburg-Strelitz ; 20, Holstein-Oldenberg ; 21, Anhalt-Dessau ; 22, Anhalt-Bernburg ; 23, Anhalt-Cœthen ; 24, Schwartzberg-Rudolstadt ; 26, Hohenzollern-Hechingen ; 27, Lichtenstein ; 28, Hohenzollern-Sigmaringen ; 29, Waldeck ; 30, Reuss (elder branch) ; 31, Reuss (younger branch) ; 32, Schomberg-Lippe ; 33, Lippe-Detmold ; 34, Hesse-Homburg ; 35, Lubeck ; 36, Frankfort-on-the-Maine ; 37, Bremen ; 38, Hamburg—the four last being free cities. Some modifications of the original confederation have since been made, but the basis of union is the same now as in 1815. Austria presides in an annual Diet, or meeting of representatives of the various states, and three or four larger powers of Germany decide by the preponderance of votes all questions deliberated upon. The objects of the German Confederation are mutual protection and defence in time of war, and adjustment of political difficulties in peace. After the peace of Paris, in 1814, the German States regained most of their sequestrated territory from French domination, and remained comparatively undisturbed till 1830, when the French Revolution, which removed Charles X., caused some revulsions beyond the Rhine, resulting, however, in no permanent political change beyond a revolution in the Netherlands, and erection of the separate kingdom of Belgium. The German confederated States are bound by articles of various treaties made in 1814–15, to assist each other against any foreign enemy, not a Germanic power, that invades German territory. If the actual German dominions of Austria be threatened by France, the German Diet must call out the military contingents of all its members, but while the war is confined to Italian soil, which, though held by Austria, is not actual German territory, the Confederation is not bound to interfere for Austria's assistance.

XXI.

It will be recollected that when Napoleon first led his armies against Russia, it was with the general understanding that, in event of triumph, he would reconstruct the nationality of Poland, which had been destroyed by the three powers of Russia, Prussia, and Austria. At the peace of Tilsit he, doubtless, might have accomplished this, but contented himself with erecting Prussian Poland, joined to other territory, into a state called the Duchy of Warsaw, under rule of the King of Saxony. Before the partition of Poland in 1773, that nation was an extensive republic, and had previously elected its kings. By the partition, 84,000 square miles of territory were divided between the three plundering powers—Austria receiving 27,000 square miles, comprising her present Gallician frontier ; Prussia getting all Polish Prussia, to the extent of 13,375 square miles ; and Russia taking the lion's share, of Livonia and other palatinates, amounting to 42,000 square miles. . . . . . The bulk of territory left to the unfortunate republic was sequestrated by a second partition in 1793, by which Russia obtained 96,500 square miles, with 3,000,000 inhabitants ; and Prussia, 22,500 square miles, with 1,136,000 inhabitants. The remnant of a Polish republic remained in Russian military possession till 1794, when KosciusKo and his fellow-patriots revolted, and proclaimed Warsaw, Cracow, Wilna, and other districts independent. Then came the short but glorious struggle of the Poles for their liberty, which, being unsuccessful, was followed by a third partition of the unhappy country. In October, 1795, the remaining country was divided, Russia taking 43,000 square miles, Prussia 21,000, and Austria 17,600, with more than 3,000,000 inhabitants between them. Thus, the three great powers not only destroyed a nationality, but were robbers, in all, to the amount of 282,000 square miles of land, thereby subjecting to monarchy more than twelve million people who had constituted a republican nation.

XXII.

The atrocious dismemberment of Poland was one of the direct outrages of despotism which evoked the spirit that became incarnated in French Revolution. The political writers of France seized upon the theme as a text for philippics against royalty, and public opinion everywhere, as far as it then could manifest itself, became excited upon the subject. The two great monarchical governments of Great Britain and France remained inactive, and saw the iniquity commenced, in 1773, without a protest ; but the French Republic of 1795, which had arisen previous to the third partition, afterward became a scourge for Russia, Austria, and Prussia. Napoleon Bonaparte declared his expeditions against Russia to be "Polish Wars," but from his first conquest, to his Moscow defeat, the nationality of Poland was made but a cat's paw to draw out republican sympathies, and the betrayed country remained in 1815, as in 1795, sequestrated between Russia, Prussia, and Austria. . . . . . . At the CONGRESS OF VIENNA, the British plenipotentiary endeavored to effect a reinstatement of Poland in her just rights, but was unsuccessful ; and the following articles, freely translated from Wheaton's notes, fixed the fate of that nation :

"Art. 1. The Duchy of Warsaw, with the exception of the provinces and districts otherwise disposed under the following articles, is reunited to the Russian Empire. It shall be irrevocably, by its constitution, possessed by his Majesty the Emperor of all the Russias, his heirs and successors in perpetuity. His majesty reserves to himself the enjoyment of a distinct administration, and interior extension, as he shall judge convenient. He will take, with his other titles, that of Czar, King of Poland, agreeably to the protocol used and set apart for the titles attached to his other possessions. Polish subjects, of Russia, Austria, and Prussia respectively, shall obtain such a *representation* and *national institutions*, regulated in accordance with the political system of each of the governments, as shall be deemed proper to accord them.

"Art. 6. The town of CRACOW, with its territory, is declared *perpetually* an independent *free city*, strictly neutral, under protection of Russia, Austria, and Poland.

"Art. 9. The courts of Russia, Austria, and Prussia engage to respect, and cause to be respected, forever, the neutrality of the free city of Cracow and its territory. *No armed force shall ever be introduced therein under any pretence whatsoever.* In return, it is understood, and expressly stipulated, that no asylum or protection in the territory of Cracow, shall ever be accorded to runaways, deserters, or fugitives from law, belonging to the country of either of the high powers aforesaid, and that, under a demand for extradition from competent authorities, such individuals shall be arrested and given up without delay, under good escort, to guards charged to receive them on the frontier."

A constitutional charter was granted by Alexander to the new kingdom of Poland, on the 15th November, 1815, by provisions of which the Russian emperor was to be its sovereign, and crowned in Warsaw, and was to take an oath to observe the charter. The Polish nation was to have a perpetual representation composed of the king and a diet, in which body the legislative power, including that of taxation, was to be vested. A distinct military organization, coinage, and distinctions were to be preserved to this Polish kingdom, united with the Russian Empire.

XXIII.

In 1830, following the example of the French and Belgians, Polish patriots attempted a revolution against Russia, which awakened sympathy throughout the world, but was unsuccessful ; and in 1832, the Emperor Nicholas established an organic statute for the kingdom of Poland, by which it was declared to be perpetually incorporated with Russia, the Polish diet being abolished, and a governor-general placed over the country. By this proceeding on the part of Russia, the TREATY OF VIENNA was violated by a power that had been a party to it. Russia's breach of faith was followed by that of Austria, in 1836, when that government sent troops to the *Free City of Cracow*, which composed an independent state, as provided by treaty, of 51,000 square miles, and a population of 110,000, on the Vistula. Cracow's representative government was considered dangerous in Austrian neighborhood, and was therefore subverted, and the *Free City* became, like Warsaw, a sacrifice to despotism, in direct contravention of the Vienna treaties. The British Government protested against these violations of charters ; but as it declined to adopt hostile proceedings in order to compel a respect for treaties, the royal continental spoilers remained in possession of their new plunder. . . . . . Poland has since been the NIOBE of Europe, her tears shed through exiles on every soil, her complaints made to every people, and her fate remembered as a heavy debt to be sometime settled, with Russia, Austria, and Prussia. Her final destruction exhibits but one of the broken pledges of those powers whose representatives "settled the peace of Europe," in 1815. The constitutions of Warsaw and of Cracow were, without doubt, annihilated in accordance with those secret articles of agreement entered into, the 22d November, 1822, and appended, as before mentioned, to the Holy Alliance treaty, of 1815. By these secret articles, the REAL OBJECTS of the Alliance were defined to be THE DESTRUCTION OF REPRESENTATIVE GOVERNMENT, AND THE SUPPRESSION OF THE LIBERTY OF THE PRESS IN ALL EUROPE. The provisions of this infamous league of monarchs against the people, are as follows :

"SECRET TREATY OF VERONA.

"The undersigned, specially authorized to make some additions to *The Treaty of the Holy Alliance*, after having exchanged their respective credentials, have agreed as follows:

"Art. 1. The high contracting powers, being convinced that the system of *representative* government is equally as *incompatible* with the monarchical principle as the maxim of the sovereignty of the people with the divine right, engage mutually, in the most solemn manner, to use all their efforts to *put an end* to the system of *representative* government, in whatever country it may exist in Europe, and to prevent its being introduced in those countries where it is not yet known.

"Art. 2. As it cannot be doubted that the *liberty* of the *press* is the most powerful means used by the pretended supporters of the rights of nations, to the detriment of those of princes, the high contracting parties promise reciprocally to adopt all proper measures to *suppress* it, not only in their own states, but also in the rest of Europe.

"Art. 3. Convinced that the principles of religion contribute most powerfully to keep nations in the state of passive obedience which they owe to their princes, the high contracting parties declare it to be their intention to sustain, in their respective states, those measures which the clergy may adopt, with the aim of ameliorating their own interests, so intimately connected with the preservation of the authority of princes; and the contracting powers join in offering their thanks to the Pope, for what he has already done for them, and solicit his constant coöperation in their views of subverting the nations.

"Art. 4. The situation of Spain and Portugal unite unhappily all the circumstances to which this treaty has particularly reference. The high contracting parties, in confiding to France the care of putting an end to them, engage to assist her in the manner which may the least compromit them with their own people and the people of France, by means of a subsidy on the part of the two empires, of twenty millions of francs every year, from the date of the signature of this treaty to the end of the war.

"Art. 5. In order to establish in the Peninsula the order of things which existed before the revolution of Cadiz, and to insure the entire execution of the articles of the present treaty, the high contracting parties give to each other the reciprocal assurance, that as long as their views are not fulfilled, rejecting all other ideas of utility, or other measures to be taken, they will address themselves with the shortest possible delay, to all the authorities existing in their states and to all their agents in foreign countries, with the view to establish connections tending toward the accomplishment of the objects proposed by this treaty.

"Art. 6. This treaty shall be renewed with such changes as new circumstances may give occasion for, either at a new Congress, or at the court of one of the contracting parties, as soon as the war with Spain shall be terminated.

"Art. 7. The present treaty shall be ratified, and the ratifications exchanged at Paris within the space of six months.

"Made at Verona, the 22d Nov. 1822.

(Signed)   "For *Austria*, METTERNICH;
"*France*, CHATEAUBRIAND;
"*Prussia*, BERNSTET;
"*Russia*, NESSELRODE."

XXIV.

I shall now glance at the Danubian Valley, in order to show the relations which Russia bears to the principalities of MOLDAVIA, WALLACHIA, BULGARIA, SERVIA, and other extensive districts lying between the sovereignties of Russia, Austria, and Turkey, and claimed by turns to belong to each. The country comprised in those principalities is blessed by temperate climate and fruitful soil, and was anciently traversed by the land commerce of all the world exchanging between Europe and the East. Under the Roman Emperor Trajan, it was the seat of flourishing communities; and under Charlemagne, the Danubian Valley became a great thoroughfare between Constantinople and Paris. It is now, in many parts, a wilderness, only semi-civilized anywhere, and maintaining feudalism and servitude as in the dark ages. The nobles, or *boyards*, are wealthy and luxurious; the peasantry, oppressed and ignorant. Violence, anarchy, misrule, despotism ⁊e changed the face of nature in this beautiful valley of the Danube, ⁊ ⁊ù has become an abode more fit for beasts than for men. But Russian dip⁊ ⁊acy has seen in the character of the inhabitants its proper material for a ⁊bject population, and Russian ambition has for centuries disputed with Turk⁊y the possession of these Principalities, as an assurance that Constantinople i⁊self must afterward succumb. If a general war shall *now* convulse Europe, we may look for a bold push on the part of the Czar to appropriate, at the least, a *share* of the Danubian Valley. In order, therefore, to comprehend the present legitimate possession of the Principalities, it may be well to consult a few articles of the Treaty of Adrianople, in 1820, between Russia and the Ottoman Empire:

"TREATY OF PEACE BETWEEN RUSSIA AND TURKEY. SIGNED AT ADRIANOPLE, SEPTEMBER **14,** 1829.

"In the name of God Almighty.

"His imperial majesty, the most high and most mighty emperor and autocrat of all the Russias, and his highness the most high and most mighty emperor of the Ottomans, animated with an equal desire to put an end to the calamities of war, and to establish, on a solid and immutable basis, peace, friendship, and good harmony between their empires, have resolved, with a common accord, to intrust this salutary work to," etc.

[Here follow the names and titles of the different plenipotentiaries on both sides.]

"Art. I. All enmity and all differences which have subsisted hitherto between the two empires shall cease from this day, as well on land as on sea, and there shall be in perpetuity peace, friendship, and good intelligence, between his majesty the emperor and padishah of all the Russias, and his highness the padishah of the Ottomans, their heirs and successors to the throne, as well as between their respective empires. The two high contracting parties will devote their particular attention to prevent all that might cause misunderstandings to revive between their respective subjects. They will scrupulously fulfill all the conditions of the present treaty of peace, and will watch, at the same time, lest it should be infringed in any manner, directly or indirectly.

"Art. II. His majesty the emperor and padishah of all the Russias, wishing to give to his highness the emperor and padishah of the Ottomans a pledge of the sincerity of his friendly disposition, restores to the Sublime Porte the principality of Moldavia, with all the boundaries which it had before the commencement of the war to which this present treaty has put an end.

"His imperial majesty also restores the principality of Wallachia, the Banat of Crayova, Bulgaria, and the country of Dobridge, from the Danube as far as the sea, together with Silistria, Hirsova, Matzia, Isakiya, Toulza, Babadag, Bazardjik, Varna, Pravedy, and the other towns, burghs, and villages, which it contains, the whole extent of the Balkan, from Emine Bouroun as far as Kazan, and all the country from the Balkans as far as the sea with Siliminea, Jomboli, Aidos, Karnabat, Missanovica, Akhioly, Bourgas, Sizopolis Kirkkilissi, the city of Adrianople, Lule Bourgas, and all the towns, burghs, and villages, and in general all places which the Russian troops have occupied in Roumelia.

"Art. III. The Pruth shall continue to form the limit of the two empires, from the point where the river touches the territory of Moldavia to its junction with the Danube; from that spot the frontier line will follow the course of the Danube as far as the mouth of the St. George, so that leaving all the islands formed by the different arms of that river, in possession of Russia, the right bank shall remain, as formerly, in the possession of the Ottoman Porte. Nevertheless, it is agreed that this right bank shall remain uninhabited from the point where the arm of St. George separates itself from that of the Souline, to a distance of two hours from the river, and that no establishment of any kind shall be formed there, any more than on the islands which shall remain in possession of the court of Russia, where, with the exception of the quarantines which may be established there, it shall not be allowed to make any other establishment or fortification. The merchant vessels of the powers shall have the liberty of navigating the Danube in all its course; and those which bear the Ottoman flag shall have free entrance into the mouth of the Keli and Souline, that of St. George remaining common to the ships of war and merchant vessels of the two contracting powers. But the Russian ships of war, when ascending the Danube, shall not go beyond the point of its junction with the Pruth.

"Art. IV Georgia, Imeritia, Mingrela, and several other provinces of the Caucasus, having been for many years and in perpetuity united to the empire of Russia, and that empire having besides, by the treaty concluded with Persia, at Tourkmantchaï, on the 10th of February, 1828, acquired the Khanats of Erivan and of Naktchivan, the two high contracting powers have recognized the necessity of establishing between their respective states, on the whole of that line, a well determined frontier, capable of preventing all future discussion. They have equally taken into consideration the proper means to oppose insurmountable obstacles to the incursions and depredations which the neighboring tribes hitherto committed, and which have so often compromised the relations of friendship and good feeling between the two empires; consequently it has been agreed upon, to consider, henceforward, as the frontiers between the territories of the imperial court of Russia, and those of the sublime Ottoman Porte in Asia, the line which, following the present limit of the Gouriel from the Black Sea, ascends as far as the border of Imeritia, and from thence, in the straightest direction, as far as the point where the frontiers of the Pachaliks of Akhaltzik and of Kars meet those of Georgia, leaving in this manner to the north of, and within that line, the town of Akhaltzik and the fort of Khalinalick, at a distance of not less than two hours.

"All the countries situate to the south and west of this line of demarkation towards the Pachaliks of Kars and Trebisond, together with the major part of the Pachalik of Akhaltzik shall remain in perpetuity under the domination of the Sublime Porte, whilst those which are situated to the north and east of the said line toward Georgia, Imeritia, and the Gouriel, as well as all the littoral of the Black Sea, from the mouth of the Kouben, as far as the port of St. Nicholas inclusively under the domination of the Emperor of Russia. In consequence, the imperial court of Russia gives up and restores to the Sublime Porte the remainder of the Pachalik of Akhaltzik, the town and the Pachalik of Kars, the town and Pachalik of Bayazid, the town and Pachalik of Erzeroum, as well as all the places occupied by the Russian troops, and which may be out of the above mentioned line.

"In virtue," etc.

(Signed)	"Count ALEXIS ORLIF.
	Count J. PHALEN.
(Signed)	DIEBITSCH ZABALKANSKY."

X.

The French Revolution of 1830, resulting in the expulsion of Charles X. and election of Louis Philippe, was the signal for disturbances in various parts of Europe. Within six months afterward, a Spanish insurrection took place, but was suppressed; the Belgians revolted against Holland, and achieved their independence; the Poles made a bold but fruitless effort for liberty; all the German States bordering on the Rhine were convulsed; the King of Saxony fled from his capital; the Duke of Brunswick was driven from his government, his palace being fired by the populace; and even in Denmark, and in Austria, manifestations of revolution alarmed the reigning monarchs. . . . . ITALY, since 1815, had been suffering under various oppressions. Even Sardinia, her most liberal state, had relapsed into ultra-monarchical usages. By a decree issued in December, 1817, the King of Sardinia reëstablished feudal tenures and primogenitive rights, as they existed previous to the French Revolution ; in order, as the declaration ran, to "maintain in the class which by its peculiar institution stands nearest to the throne, and whose especial duty it is to watch over its defence, that lustre and inheritance of glory which form its noblest prerogative." Such retrogressions as this awoke popular agitation at different periods between 1815 and 1825. The military power of Austria was exerted repeatedly to prevent a universal rising. That Austrian power, always irksome to Italians, had not relaxed in severity since its restoration by Vienna Treaties. It was forced, more than once, during a series of years, to measure itself against patriotic outbreaks ; and, even before 1830, two revolutionary movements, at two extremities of the peninsula, almost re-nationalized Italians in spite of oppression. Those movements ended without bloodshed or violence, because a hereditary prince was wise enough to place himself in advance of each ; but both were fruitless in respect to securing any real freedom. The experiment of trusting their cause to *royal* revolutionists, sufficed only to satisfy the Italian people of their folly. Italy remained, as before, the domain of princes, but not the home for patriots. The yoke of Hapsburg and the Bourbons (as well as that of Papal power, half shaken off in 1830), grew heavier to bear during the second quarter of our century than were all the burdens imposed by the wars and ambition of Bonaparte in the first quarter. The French conqueror elevated even while he enchained ; he liberalized, educated, and strengthened Italy, even while he imposed his dynasties on her states. Austria, on the other hand, in enslaving the country, degraded its people under petty tyrannies, and weakened their mental and physical resources, by coupling ignorance with bondage. Her police, her censorships, her proscriptions, and confiscations, kept down the Italian mind, while they oppressed the body politic, till at length, on the accession of Pius IX. to the popedom, the first liberalizing measures of that pontiff aroused a spirit of nationality throughout all Italy. In 1847, disturbances occurred in Tuscany, Lucca, Messina, Milan, and other points of the peninsula. Pius IX. appeared to Italian patriots the destined deliverer of their country, and his progressive reforms of ancient abuses enlisted sympathy and admiration in every civilized country. In November, 1847, a demonstration in favor of the new ideas was made in Naples, which was suppressed, after bloodshed, by the government. Throughout the Lombardo-Venetian Kingdom agitation continued to increase, and the people petitioned Austria for liberal changes in administration. Austria replied by pouring new forces into her Italian provinces. . . . . The year 1848 opened with a revolution in the Neapolitan Kingdom ; a grant to Palermo and Sicily of the Constitution of 1812 ; the erection of a constitutional government in Tuscany ; a proclamation of liberal ideas by the Sardinian king, and outbreaks throughout all Austrian Italy. These proceedings were followed by the establishment of democratic institutions in Naples, the king declaring himself dependent upon his people. Other popular insurrections followed, in rapid succession. CHARLES ALBERT, King of Sardinia, then placed himself at the head of revolution, and proclaimed Italian nationality. He crossed the Ticino at the head of 100,000 patriots, drove the Austrians from Lombardy and Venetia, and declared Italy independent. . . . . But monarchical reaction speedily took place, and Austrian power gathered itself to check the advance of democratic ideas. The

King of Naples, after having yielded reforms with solemn pledges to his people, was the first sovereign to commit an act of treachery. After having obtained, by his professions of liberalism, the disarming of the Civic Guard, he armed the beggars and brigands of Naples, and gave up her patriotic citizens to violence and plunder. An army of *lazzaroni*, infuriated by drink and bribes, rose at his instigation, and reëstablished royal power, after a general pillage and massacre of the people. The triumph of Ferdinand at Naples was succeeded by an irruption of Austrian troops on emancipated Lombardy. General Radetzky, at the head of a powerful army, encountered Charles Albert at NOVARA, March 23, 1849, dispersed the Italian army, and reorganized Austrian government in Milan. Charles Albert then resigned his crown to his son, the present King of Sardinia. . . . . ROME, under her reforming Pope Pius, had likewise experienced mischances. The pontiff, after granting various reforms to his people, grew uneasy at the spread of revolution, and attempted to nullify his liberal action. Roman patriotism became alarmed, and the Pope's prime minister, Rossi, was murdered. The Pope himself abandoned the capital, to take shelter at Gaeta, under protection of the Neapolitan king. Rome was at once declared a republic, and a provisional government organized, with Mazzini, Avezzani, and Garribaldi at the head of affairs, as Triumvirate. The Pope, on his part, issued an appeal for aid to all Catholic powers, and the French Government responded by advancing an army over the borders toward Rome. An investment of that city by the French intervention-troops, under Oudinot, shortly followed ; and on July 30, 1849, the Roman Republic fell, after a gallant defence against superior numbers and arms. . . . . The reaction of Despotism was completed by the capture of Brescia and Genoa, by Generals Haynau and Marmora, and the reduction of Venice ; and, after an arduous siege, Sardinia was forced to make terms, and Italy remained, as before, in the hands of her oppressors, the Bourbons and Hapsburgs.

XXV.

Meantime, after abortive struggles in 1830, the German States proper relapsed into toleration of their confederated system, under lead of Austria and Prussia ; and thus continued till the startling movements of 1848 were participated in throughout all the German land. Bavaria was first to proclaim a free press and progressive representation ; Schleswig-Holstein revolted from Danish government ; Bohemian deputies met, and framed a liberal constitution ; Hungary demanded and obtained from Austria an independent constitution ; and a parliament of German States convened at Frankfort, to take measures for reorganization and a German national unity, with free institutions. . . The people rose in Dresden, Baden, Dusseldorf, Breslau, and other places. The Austrian imperial dynasty was driven from Vienna, and the people of Berlin raised barricades and forced their king to agree to a constitution, and accept the tri-color as an emblem of popular sovereignty. For several months, Germany thrilled with the excitement of recovered independence, and the Frankfort Parliament was recognized as a national head. Ferdinand of Austria abdicated in favor of his nephew. Louis Kossuth and Count Bathiany revolutionized Hungary, and made head against Jellachich, the governor of Croatia, who had raised an army in favor of the emperor. . . . . . The reaction then commenced. Vienna was assaulted and taken by an imperial force under Gen. Windischgratz, and the prince Francis Joseph was declared emperor ; the Prussian king broke faith with his people, and placed Berlin under martial law ; the Frankfort parliament was dispersed and some of its

members shot ; and finally, republican manifestations were suppressed everywhere but in Hungary. In that country, a gallant resistance was maintained
three months longer by the influence of enthusiastic leaders, Kossuth, Dem-
binski, Bem, Klapka, and Georgey, till the last-mentioned general, receiving
the supreme command, surrendered 30,000 men to a Russian general. The
consequence of this treachery was the suppression of the Hungarian revolution,
and the total overthrow of the popular cause throughout Europe. The dynastic reaction continued, and rolled back upon republican France, preparing her
for events which followed rapidly, till the imperial coronation of Louis Napoleon, in 1850, put a final period to the hopes and dreams of republican unity in
Europe. From that time to the present, Germany has remained quiet, and
France grown accustomed to the rule of Napoleon III., until he now leads her
in the paths of Napoleon I. through Italy.

OBJECTS OF A DYNASTIC WAR.

I.

MEN talk variously concerning the anticipated drama, and of that leading
character of its expected scenes, whose temples wear the bloody diadem of
imperial France ; for, as yet, both old and new countries are in doubt regarding the policy of Napoleon III. It is not sufficient that, as mere spectators of
a ten years' political panorama, we survey the fortunes of this monarch since
1848, nor that we recall his earlier *escapades* at Strasbourg and Boulogne; that
we remember the misgivings of patriots which counselled his ostracism from
the Republic under Lamartine ; that we recollect how, through reaction of imperial traditions, he was returned as a deputy to the National Assembly ; or
that, finally, we reflect upon the Bonapartist sentiment which elevated him to
the French Presidency—a sentiment which pre-supposed a committal of the
candidate's sentiments to hostility against the English government. If we
trace his tortuous policy, step by step, in climbing from obscurity to imperial
eminence, we behold him always enveloped in a fog of deception, that, like
the cloudy robe of a sorcerer during incantation, waxes darker with each new
spell, more cunningly concealing the secret machinery. By his famous *coup
d'état*, a stroke of mingled treachery and boldness, he achieved the same position
that his uncle reached through similar means. By the terrorism of his African
generals he paralyzed the national councils of 1850, as Napoleon I. had paralyzed those of 1795 by the armed partisanship of his brother Lucien. While
he broke the oaths sworn on the Republic's altar, he again mimicked his uncle
by crowning himself an emperor ; and yet we find him oblivious, almost
instantly of the souvenirs of Waterloo, and becoming an ally of England in a
Quixotic war to uphold the sham of Turkish nationality. The nephew, and
avowed representative of that Bonaparte whose very existence the continental
and island sovereigns had declared forfeited in their proclamation of March
14, 1815 ; the successor of that Titan who died chained to a rock, gnawed to
the last by the vulture of British persecution—hastened to fraternize with the
ancient enemy, who had humbled France at Waterloo, and dictated her des-

tiny within the walls of Paris. Forgetful, apparently, that he owed his first advancement under the republic to a carefully-encouraged popular belief in his desire and ability to carry out his uncle's schemes against England, this arch-diplomatist became the friend of "perfidious Albion," and squire of dames to England's queen and court.

II.

But apparent fraternization of France with England, remained, after all, only apparent ! On the one hand was a government bound by every national recollection to oppose its island rival ; on the other were classes and communities imbued with an ancestral jealousy regarding continental encroachments. On the French side, the *prestige* of Lamartine had waned from the hour when he rebuked the *drapeaux rouges* of a war with England ; on the side of Great Britain were heard the warnings of Wellington against French intrigue, and his prediction of disastrous consequences to follow faith in Louis Napoleon. With these lights of history to direct us in contemplating an alliance that made the two governments so apparently fraternal, we might, perhaps, discover beneath the surface of affairs some concealed machinery to account for many strange problems of a mighty dynastic game of chess. It is known to historic students that in the line of policy inaugurated by Napoleon I., no federal relations with Great Britain could ever find a place. The random diplomacy with which the astute Corsican often chose to cover his more deeply-meditated schemes, did, more than once, it is true, ostensibly lean towards a cultivation of British friendship; but no analytic historian has maintained that an alliance with England was ever an ulterior or serious design of Bonaparte. Contemporaneous facts, on the other hand, testify that he, on many occasions, sought a permanent confederacy with Russia—that he was at one time on the point of effecting an offensive and defensive alliance with Alexander ; that he sought to unite himself in marriage with that emperor's sister, even though the step involved a profession of the Greek faith ; in fine, that his far-reaching policy demarked the map of Europe into two absolute dynastic divisions, one to be possessed by his own family, the other to be ruled by the Czar. On one hand was to be dynastic RUSSIA, dominating the Danubian principalities, wresting Indian dominion from Great Britain, and spreading her vast sovereignty from the Volga and Bosphorus to the Chinese seas; on the other, dynastic FRANCE, absorbing all German nationalities as far as the line which marked Sclavonic races, gallicizing Spain, Portugal, and the Italian peninsula, and consolidating French dominion from the Adriatic to the Zuyder Zee.

III.

Had the peace of Tilsit been succeeded by such harmonious results as the affectionate interview of the two emperors at first prognosticated—had the Czar's confidence in Napoleon's integrity equalled his admiration of the Corsican's brilliant military qualities, there is no reason to doubt that a course of policy would have followed the "treaty of the raft" which might have actualized the shadowy chart of continental sequestration then dimly outlined in Napoleon's master-brain. Nations would have been redistricted from the Rhine and Po to the Ganges and Yellow Sea. The old world would have been partitioned between Gaul and Muscovite, as it had formerly been divided when Byzantium and Rome were capitals of Eastern and Western Cæsars. There was to be, in effect, a new Roman world for the two modern Cæsars, frontiered much as in the ancient time. Napoleon of France and Alexander of Russia were to reënact the *rôles* of Constantine and Constantius—the first at Stamboul or St. Petersburg, the second at Paris or the Tiber's banks—reviving for their respective dynasties an empire of the East and an empire of the West. It was a magnificiently aggressive and unscrupulous scheme ; but one which, we are constrained to believe, was ardently contemplated by the First Napoleon. That Napoleon III. is a disciple of his ambitious uncle in the school of which Talleyrand was a diplomatic expert, is apparent in nothing more than this, that he has thus far skillfully veiled his own sympathy with the half-wrought purposes of him who called himself " the man of destiny." " Words," said the time-serving Prince of Benevento, " are intended to conceal thoughts ;" and no one has profited by the maxim to a greater extent than the present Emperor of France. At this hour, doubtless, he has practical plans, under apparent political indefiniteness, which may yet make real much that under the first empire was theoretic.

IV.

With Russia as permanent ally, the French government might ere long proclaim with impunity the principle of autocratic rule ? Throughout her entire history, France has enjoyed greater national prosperity in proportion as her destinies were controlled by absolute power. Under Charlemagne, Louis XI., Henri Quatre, Richelieu, until royal glories culminated with the fourteenth Louis and imperial power with Napoleon Bonaparte, the grandest epochs of French prosperity have been likewise periods of paramount monarchic rule. With autocratic sway exercised over spirit-broken masses, enforced by eight hundred thousand soldiers, and backed by Russian autocracy at the head of twenty million serfs, emancipated from oligarchic masters, France would be strong enough to carry out the boldest plans of Napoleon I. for the spoliation of civilized countries, and new partition of the world. Opposing Russia, Louis Napoleon would only, by strengthening liberalism, weaken the tenure of his own authority. Allied with Russia, the initiative of imperial extension taken by France in a war against Austria, could be followed up by the Czar Alexander with a renewed assault upon the Turkish " sick man." The world need not be wholly unprepared for an entire *bouleversement* of present European alliances, and a speedy awakening of the English press and people from that strange infatuation which makes them the catspaw of absolutism—the dupe of diplomatic artifices, and perhaps a predestined sacrifice to his imperial *manes* whose " ghost walks unavenged" around the Invalides of Paris.

V.

It requires no superior discernment to foresee possibilities ; and on possibilities and probabilities prudent men may fittingly speculate. It is *possible* that, with Alexander of Russia for his coadjutor, Louis Napoleon might desire to intrench himself impregnably against popular revolution, and enact his uncle's drama of empire to the letter—controlling meantime the elements of Spanish and Italian nationality for future consolidation, as in the days of Joseph and Murat. It is *possible* that, with Louis Napoleon for his ally, the Emperor Alexander might wish to make good those claims to Oriental Cæsarship that were bequeathed some centuries ago to Czar Ivan Ivanowich, by the fugitive Greek monarch Alexis, whom he protected—claims afterward asserted by Empress Catherine, when she guide-marked through her realm " the road to Constantinople." It is *possible* that, with Louis Napoleon to deal with prostrate republicanism, Alexander might pursue his usurpations to the Ganges—command central Europe with his fleet, sallying from the Levant, sweep the Chinese Archipelago, and annihilate British influence from Suez to Japan. Finally, it is *possible* that the united despotisms of France and Russia might have the power to realize the worst apprehensions of Kossuth ; and if they should fail to crush out England as a nation, might at least confine her ultimately to narrow island jurisdiction. Do I conjecture these results to be possible, or suggest that warnings of Wellington concerning France, and the vaticinations of Kossuth regarding a league of tyrannies, may be worthy of recollection at the present time ? Do I hazard a doubt whether that entire game of war against Russia, levied in behalf of the "sick man" Turkey, was not, after all, a diplomatic sham on the part of Louis Napoleon—cruel and sanguinary, but still a gigantic sham ? Would I assume, for illustration, that the delays and blunders of that useless war—the obvious superiority of French arms in all important operations—the lack of unanimity in councils or concert in action—all tending to enfeeble British prestige and power—might have been preconcerted problems of a stupendous game of diplomatic chess ? And should it be flippantly rejoined that such battles as Balaklava and Inkerman, such horrors as were common in trench and pest-house throughout dreary and abortive campaigns, are not the games of diplomacy which civilized nations play—I might answer that Borodinos and Eylaus, and Moscows, are the moves and mates of Alexanders and Napoleons upon the bloody board of their ambition. What were the lives of fifty thousand serfs to the lord of thirty millions, if their sacrifice insured also the depletion of Great Britain of blood and treasure, and the crippling of her energies for years to come ? What was Sevastopol as a temporarily-relinquished pawn, if the Golden Horn castle—key of the Dardanelles—may be yet a prize for the son of Nicholas ? Who shall affirm that Napoleon III. is not astute enough to have smoothed, long since, by secret diplomacy, the path of overt conquest which he will ere long pursue ? Who shall deny that he is sufficiently ambitious to dare all that his uncle conceived, but survived not to execute ?

VI.

At this crisis of European affairs, it is not improper to consider the relations which our own country may bear to old world nations, and to observe the significant movements of those sovereignties that are naturally antagonistic to sovereignty of the people. The prospect of a definite consolidation of Russian and French interests ; the rapid growth of a Gallic party in Spain ; the skillful control of revolutionary materials in Lombardy, in order to occupy Austria with Italian war ; the initiation of a Muratist movement in Naples ; the immense naval preparations of both Russia and France, joined with French intrigue in the College of Cardinals at Rome, are signs indicative of the future, and seem to index, as an ultimate object, the creation of colossal imperial dynasties under Napoleon and Alexander. The first immolation to be made in such event would be the nationality of Austria. Austrian nationality, even now, is but a thing of "shreds and patches." Powerful in military organization, and pretensions in widely-extended territory, Austria, after all, is but the archducal domain of Hapsburgh, bloated into dropsical empire. The very incongruity of her resources has been a secret of success in keeping down so many independent peoples enslaved by her centralizing power. The regiments intended to curb Sclavonian tributaries are drafted from Magyar or German population ; German cities are garrisoned by Croats ; Hungarian villages by

Italian recruits ; Italian provinces by Bohemians, Transylvanians and Hun-
garians. Thus Austria pits race against race, and defies fraternization of
soldiers and citizens by interposing the barriers of creed, language and country
between her subjects and their guards. With her high imperial position, she has
no real national existence, and possesses no ties of blood, religion, or even local
interest to unite her various provinces. On the south, Italian subjects pant
for their lost nationality ; on the north, Sclavonic hordes claim common origin
with Russia's tribes, and acknowledge a Muscovite head of the Greek Church,
to which they are attached.

VII.

The House of Brandenburg, second Germanic power, represents no sounder
nationality at present than it did before the Peace of Utrecht, when Prussian
dukes paid homage to now-dismembered Poland. It has made acquisition of
Swedish, Silesian and Polish territory, and was the mover of so-called
German Confederation. But the treaty of Tilsit exhibited its actual weakness,
and it is doubtful whether another *Tugend-Bund* league of patriots would
uphold a dynasty which has betrayed popular trust by repeated breaches of
even a sham constitution. Nor are the smaller German states entirely free
from jealousy regarding Austria's overgrown bulk, or the enlarging ambition
of Prussia. " What have we to do," demanded the "address of Rhenish
Bavaria to its king," as far back as 1832—" what have we to do with
Austria, that old, musty, worm-eaten, hollow trunk ? It will be dashed to the
ground by the worms of time, and in the storm will crush all those who seek
shelter beneath its boughs. What advantage to constitutional Bavaria can
be offered by absolute Prussia, a treacherous cane that pierces through the
hand which would find support by leaning on it ?" Regarding the real
aspects of German politics, the question might be asked, What is meant by
German confederation for independence now invoked by Austrian partisans?
What traditional allegiance to this or that power can effect the nationalization
of Germany, now separated into thirty-eight, as it was formerly pieced into
more than three hundred distinct sovereignties? In what actual German
cause can the Landstürm be now summoned by alarmed princes ? The year
1848 has more souvenirs for popular sympathy than all " hereditary " and
" legitimate " claims of duchies, margravates, principalities and lordships, in
the oligarchic *plenum* of a Frankfort Diet. With these souvenirs, too, are
mingled other recollections and associations. Millions of expatriated *Germans*,
on *this* side of the Atlantic, are casting back, on every homeward-blowing
wind, ten thousand novel ideas, energetic suggestions and hopeful associations,
that were born of liberty and independence in backwoods of America, and
are destined to expand and take form of deeds in old forests of Saxony,
wildernesses of Sclavonia and fruitful borders of Rhine-washed France.
These consequences in good time will be felt, when myriad silent words, sealed
in home-letters from emigrants, shall have been weighed, studied over and
incorporated with awakening mind of thoughtful men and women, from the
Scheldt to the Vistula.

VIII.

Meantime, it is true, the enemies of liberalism are not insensible to the progress of ideas. Never was grasp of aggression upon suffering relaxed from
mere volition of aggressor. No parturition of humanity or nature takes place

without pain and struggle. Men who think that the knotty problem of a nation's capacity to govern itself—tangled and crossed in hands of Greeks, Romans, Italians, French, during centuries—is now unravelled and flexile, binding fasces of American States, and ready to embrace old-world federated commonwealths as well—are too sanguine. Certain Gordian intricacies of the ancient knot have been sword-severed, but other intertwistings and convolutions must still be sword-cut many times, ere strands and fibres lie paralleled, fit to retie and thereafter girdle bundles of free men in bodies politic. Coils of cord and crooks of thread—bound up for ages with prison-thongs, strangling-ropes, tackling of gun-carriages, scourge-lashes—all these must come out of that hard, compact old Gordian knot which yet puzzles peoples and princes. Monarchs and divine-right claimants to ownership of realms cannot cordially assist the enfranchisement of individual men or nations, but must rather obey instincts and traditions in utter opposition to liberal ideas. Hapsburgs, Brandenburgs, Bourbons, Braganzas, Hanovers, Holsteins, Guelfs, and Ghibelines —rent-rolled or landless, crowned or exiled—have all dynastic interests to uphold against innovation of democracy. Lions, bears, bi-cephalous eagles, hawks, or dung-hill cocks—whatsoever beasts and birds are blazoned on royal banners —hold that in common which makes them creatures of prey. The people have been purveyors for their appetites since the days of Pharaohs and Nimrods, and they themselves have, from time to time, made quarries of one another, whereby the greater absorbed the less—strong nationalities devoured feeble ones. As in old time, so in our day. The royal brutes measure strength and appetites. Some are to eat—others to be eaten !

IX.

Behold the map of European battle-plain, south, bordered by coast-line from British Channel to Adriatic Sea, and thence through Dardanelles and Bosphorus ; inland, then, to Odessa and the Danube, and westward to the Gulf of Finland. On this extended field, armies of France and Russia might operate toward common centres, compressing Austria and the Principalities, Prussia and German States, within contractile walls of encroaching hostilities. The southern continent becomes, meantime, a theatre of revolutionary action from Tiber to Tagus. Alps and Pyrenees renew the old-time thunders that echoed from Millesimo to Jena, marking Napoleonic footsteps. Naples, Milan, Venice, Rome herself, quiver with life-like spasms of revolutionary galvanism. Faint-hearted Pio Nono ! whose hand once rested, in benediction, on the radiant brow of Italian Regeneration : whose feet once trod the shining pathway of a world's enfranchisement, but tottered, deviated, and sunk, mired in half-way bog and quicksand, till freedom's torch went out within his hand, and faith in man and God gave way to fear of tyrants !—Pio Nono may be the last priestly dweller in the Vatican—last Pontiff-King of Rome ! His triple crown may pass from him to glitter on a younger, doubtless craftier head !—perhaps to press the temples of a Bonaparte, and flash its sacred light on zealous worshippers in lands where mother church still holds her rule unquestioned. What web of subtle scheming may involve the New World in its future woof ! What far-cast horoscopes of strange events may cross our freedom with their baleful lines ! A Bonaparte on the throne of France, and a Bonaparte cardinal raised to St. Peter's chair, would present a combination fraught with interest to humanity. No rheumy dotard dragged from obscure cell by plotting cardinal-electors, to do their will as papal puppet in the Quirinal ; but a shrewd, ambitious, ener-

4

gizing Bonaparte, backed by the power of France, may be the next pope, who
will, perhaps, stretch out his vigorous arms to grasp the sovereignty of conscience in two worlds.   It is felt that Rome must soon be abandoned as a
papal seat, and that the reign of Pius IX. may soon be terminated.   The air
of Italy is hot with fevered liberalism, that pants for national expression.
Consolidation of her long-sundered states—a dream of Machiavelli, a hope of
Charles Albert, a desire of Napoleon I.—may become a *fait accompli* under Napoleon III.   In that event, the spiritual head of Catholicism cannot hope to
retain his present temporal dominions, and if his successor be indeed a scion of
the house of Bonaparte—a member at present of the hierarchy—some new and
stronger domain must be sought, further, perhaps, than Avignon.   Where,
in such case, could warmer welcome greet the Vicar of St. Peter, than in the
clime which Columbus gave to Castile and Leon ?—in South America, where
Catholic States would, doubtless, vie with one another, proffering fealty and
devotion to the head of the ancient church ?   And wherever, on plateaus of
Andes, or plains of Mexico, the transplanted papacy might locate itself, it
would receive fresh blood and redoubled strength from the support of ten millions of Catholic votaries, faithful and obedient in proportion to their simplicity
of faith.   A hundred mixed races and tribes of our South American Continent, from
Terra del Fuego to the Rio Gila, would hail the erection of a Popedom in their
midst as the earnest of a grand Catholic nationality of Americo-Iberian descendants.   One thing is certain, in reference to the popedom—whether it shall find
future seat on Eastern or Western Continent—that the present ruler of France
will have chief voice in the naming of a successor to Pio Nono.   Whether or not
he shall decide to raise his priestly kinsman to St. Peter's chair, there is
little doubt that he will exercise influence over the college of cardinals, in
naming the candidate who shall be chosen.   Whoso imperial France wills to
wear the tiara, few cardinal electors will care to oppose.

X.

"Italia for Italians !" is at present an all-sufficient watchword.   Restoration
of Imperial Rome is a grand promise for the nineteenth century.   The Iron
Crown of Lombardy may bind Napoleón's brows once more.   Genoa, the proud ;
Venice, new-wedded Queen of Adriatic ;   Florence, the beautiful ;   Milan ;   Ferrara ;   ancient Piacenza, whence another invading German shall again be driven ;
Rome, with rebuilded Colosseum, new-palaced Capitoline Hill, drained Pontine
Marshes, restored Campagna; Naples, with Capreæ renovated for senile dalliances
of a French Tiberius ;—all these storied localities seem to echo, heart-full of
the past, a new summons of present-age dynasties, recalling their splendors ;
till blare of trumpets and thunder of cannon are drowned in the shout of
regenerated Italy ! . . . . . .   Amid such a turmoil of popular warlike enthusiasm as exists in Italy now, the vicarial prince of peace and custodian of St.
Peter's keys may soon find himself imperilled.   Vatican, Quirinal, Sistine Chapel,
Basilica, will remain monuments of a mighty hierarchy of the past in Italy ;
while St. Peter's shrine, new glorified, but no longer supremely sanctified, may
echo in a few years to a primate's, legate's, or metropolitan's voice, as did its
humbler predecessor, when holy fathers dwelt at Avignon.   But though Vice-
Pope, or simple Bishop of Rome, hereafter occupy the Seven-Hilled City, as
before the age of Zachary, the voice of a Papal Head from this western continent, would rule his European flock quite as effectually as they are now ruled
by a pope upheld with French bayonets.   It would be a strange but impres-

sive episode in the Napoleonic march of empire, to behold the trembling form of Papacy abandoning a troubled focus of Italian Revolution, to seek vitality and strength among faithful Roman Catholics of Spanish America, as Braganza's threatened dynasty once fled from the Tagus to Brazil. It is no startling proposition to advance, that a new Napoleonic Pope may plant St. Peter's chair amid the Andes or upon snow-headed Orizaba ; erect a visible altar of the One Unbroken Roman Church, where Manco Capac lifted idolatrous sun-disc, or where fierce Mexitli called for victims on his awful Teocalli. Cuzco and Tenochtitlan ! Peru and Mexico ! are both centres of unshaken faith in Papal supremacy ! Either of them would be a heart-core of devotion to the faith whereof St. Peter's representative is earthly head.

XI.

Looking beyond such an event—if, indeed, the Providence of Nations shall not overrule its accomplishment—the people of North American States might find matter of alarm for the future. If a consolidation of Spanish American States, by whatever means, shall ever be effected under religious national auspices, a powerful, and perhaps aggressive neighbor might threaten our own Republic. At the present time, indeed, if some absorbing motive, such as religious fanaticism, were to unite South American communities with those of Yucatan and Mexico, a dangerous weight would be thrown into the scale against us. . . . . . . If Mexico were now a consolidated power, in alliance with France and Russia, for an aggressive war on the basis of the Treaty of Vienna against popular institutions, her means of mischief would be infinite, feeble as they now appear. Russia and France, in alliance against Great Britain, and threatening our own Republic, might. assault us in vital spots, without a capability of defence on our part. A fleet and army, approaching from Russian possessions on the Pacific, where already exists the extensive war-depot of Sitka, might soon overrun the Hudsons Bay British colonies, and descend upon our undefended Oregon country ; whilst a French force might simultaneously assist Mexico to regain California and contiguous territories. There is foundation for wise uneasiness in any European intermeddling on our continent ; and an attempted protectorate of Mexico, or even Nicaragua, by France, ought to alarm the watchfulness of our government in its very inception. Should the United States ever be called upon to assist Great Britain, in a war for liberal institutions against despotic encroachments of France and Russia, it might be remembered that we have an immense seaboard open to descent from the fleets of hostile maritime powers.

THE BALANCE OF POWER IN EUROPE.

I.

To an unprejudiced student of history, who recalls European events for a century and a half, it must appear that dynastic ambition has been the prime mover of all political agitation, including revolutionary changes.   After the Peace of Utrecht, in 1713, which apparently settled many vexed questions, claims to Austrian possessions were advanced by Prussia, Spain, Sardinia, Saxony, and Bavaria, all those powers contending that portions of their own dominions were unjustly held by the House of Hapsburgh.   A general fear of Austrian aggrandizement followed the cession of Belgium to that government by the treaty of Utrecht, and the war of the Austrian Succession, in 1740, was the ultimate result.   Prussia, assisted by France, Spain, and Bavaria, laid claim to several Silesian duchies, and succeeded in obtaining all Silesia, whilst Spain received the duchies of Parma and Guastalla, at the Peace of Aix-la-Chapelle in 1748. . . . . The Seven Years' War broke out next between Prussia, and the combined powers of Austria, France, and Russia, while at the same time, a protracted conflict raged between France, Spain, Portugal, and Great Britain, involving colonies of those nations in America. . . . . The Seven Years' War brought out Russia as a first class power.   Already, her empire had been augmented in Europe by the wresting of several Baltic provinces from Sweden.   Prussia, also, enlarged her borders, by depriving Sweden of a portion of Pomerania ; Hanover increased in importance by obtaining Bremen and Verdes out of the bankruptcy of Sweden, after Charles XII. . . . . From the close of the Seven Years' War, 1763, to the French Revolution of 1789, projects of dynastic aggrandizement occupied the cabinets of leading European powers; and those projects culminated in the great International Crime which partitioned Poland between Russia, Austria, and Prussia.   In violation of all treaties, of all principles of justice, an ancient constitutional state was destroyed, and a people who had, as Christian warriors, repeatedly saved Europe from Mahammedan invasion, became denationalized and outcast as wanderers without a country.   This gigantic outrage unsettled the actual Balance of Europe, though it assumed to have only equalized the power of its perpetrators.   It inspired all the minor German nationalities with profound apprehensions of their own peril, should tripartite arrangements of leading powers be aimed at their coveted territories.   They were disposed, therefore, to welcome, rather than repel the Revolutionary movements, which promised them protection by a confederation of peoples against dynasties.   Thus the fate of Poland served as a warning for other states, and her expatriated children, spreading throughout Christendom, became, as it were, an army of martyrs, preaching a democratic crusade against the tyrannies which balanced crowns against the rights of man. . . . . Then followed Republican triumphs of France, and a consolidation of nationalities during the early career of Bonaparte, till an evil spirit of ambition took possession of that man, and from being the Representative of Peoples, he became the mere ringleader of a herd of kings.

II.

Napoleon's Empire and Napoleon's Fall passed like phantasmagoria, and then "legitimate" monarchs returned to their thrones, unrebuked by the past, unheedful of its lessons.   Great Britain, France, Austria, Prussia, and

Russia, agreed upon their Holy Alliance, and Spain, in 1817, added her consent (previously withheld) to Vienna Treaties, in consideration of the following stipulations concluded at Paris, on the 10th of June of that year, by which a portion of Italian territory was secured by reversion to the Spanish Bourbon dynasty.

TREATY OF 1817, CONCERNING PARMA, PIACENZA, AND GUASTALLA.

" In the name of the Most Holy and Indivisible Trinity.' Having recognized that the motive which has induced her Catholic Majesty to withhold her consent to the treaty, signed in the Congress at Vienna on the 9th of June, 1815, as well as that of Paris of the 20th of November of the said year, consists in the desire of seeing fixed—by the unanimous consent of the Powers which were appealed to—the application of the 99th article of the said treaty of the 9th of June, and in consequence of the revision of the Duchies of Parma, Piacenza, and Guastalla, after the decease of her Majesty, Madame the Archduchess Marie Louise, that the adhesion above mentioned was necessary to complete the general assent to the transactions upon which the political interests and the peace of Europe are principally founded.

" That her Catholic Majesty, persuaded of that truth, and animated by the same principles as her august allies, has by her full will, decided to give her consent to the said treaty in virtue of the solemn acts to that effect, signed on the 7th and 8th of June, 1817, and it having been judged convenient at the same time to satisfy the claims of Her Catholic Majesty, which concern the reversion of the said Duchies, in a manner proper to contribute advantage to the conclusion of peace, and a good understanding being happily reëstablished and existing in Europe, their imperial and royal majesties of Austria, Spain, France, Great Britain, Prussia, and Russia, have agreed to the following articles :

" Article 1. The state of actual possession of the Duchies of Parma, Piacenza and Guastalla, as well as that of the principality of Lucca, being determined by the stipulations of the 99th, 101st and 102d articles, are and remain maintained in all their force and value.

" Art. 2. The reversibility of the Duchies of Parma, Piacenza, and Guastalla, foreseen by the 99th article of the final act of the Congress of Vienna, is determined after the following manner :

" Art. 3. The Duchies of Parma, Piacenza, and Guastalla, after the decease of her Majesty the Archduchess Marie Louise, will pass in all sovereignty to her Majesty the Infanta of Spain, Marie Louise, the infant Don Carlos, Louis, his son, and their male descendants in direct and masculine line—except the districts inclosed within the States of his Imperial Majesty and Royal Highness on the left bank of the Po, which will remain in all propriety to her said Majesty, conformably to the restrictions established by the 99th article of the act of the Congress.

"Art. 4. At the same time the reversibility of the principality of Lucca, foreseen by the 102d article of the act of Congress of Vienna, will take place in the terms and under the clauses of the same article, in favor of his Imperial and Royal Highness the Grand Duke of Tuscany.

"Art. 5. Although the frontier of the Austrian States in Italy is determined by the line of the Po, it is nevertheless agreed by common consent, that the fortress of Piacenza offers a very particular interest to the system of the defence of Italy; his Imperial Majesty and Royal Highness will therefore maintain in that city, until the period of the reversions, after the extinction of the Spanish branch of the Bourbons, the pure and single right of garrison; all regular and civil rights in that city being reserved to the future sovereign of Parma; the expense and maintenance of the garrison in the city of Piacenza will be at the charge of Austria, and its force in times of peace will be amicably determined between the high parties interested, having as a rule, always in view the greatest possible comfort of the inhabitants.

" Art. 6. His Imperial Majesty and Royal Highness engages to pay to her Majesty Marie Louise, the Infanta of Spain, the sums in arrears since the 9th of June, 1815, according to the stipulations of the second paragraph of the 101st article of the act of Congress, and to continue the payment according to the same stipulations and with the same mortgage. She engages, besides, to cause to be paid to her Majesty, the Infanta, the amount of the Revenues derived from the principality of Lucca, from the same period until the moment of the entrance into possession by her Majesty, the Infanta, deduction being made of the expenses of the administration. The liquidation of these revenues will take place amicably between the high parties interested, and in case of there being a difference of opinion, they will refer to the arbitration of her most Christian Majesty.

"Art. 7. The reversion of the Duchies of Parma, Piacenza and Guastalla, in case of the extinction of the Infant Don Charles Louis, is explicitly maintained in the terms of the treaty of Aix-la-Chapelle, of 1748, and of the treaty between Austria and Sardinia of the 20th of May 1815.

" Art. 8. The present treaty drawn up in seven-fold form, will be joined to the supplementary act of the general treaty of the Congress of Vienna. It will be ratified by the high parties respectively and the ratifications will be exchanged at Paris within the space of two months, or earlier if it can be done

" In witness whereof the respective plenipotentiaries have signed the same, and thereto affixed the seal of their arms.

" Done at Paris on the 10th of the month of June, in the year of grace 1817.

Baron de VINCENT.
Count de FERNAND NUNEZ, *Duke of Monticello.*
RICHELIEU.
CHAS. STUART.
J. Compte de GOLTZ.
POZZO DI BORGO.

III.

In the following year (1818), the Five Powers of Austria, France, Great Britain, Prussia, and Russia, exchanged final ratifications at Aix-la-Chapelle. Through their representatives, Metternich, Richelieu, Castlereigh, Wellington, Hardenburgh, Bernstorff, Nesselrode, and Capo d'Istria, the great allies solemnly pledged themselves to abide by their settlement of peace, as arranged in Vienna Congress of 1815. In 1820, two years afterward, the *Secret Treaty of Verona* was framed, as I have noticed (p. 40, supra). The dynastic conspiracy against free institutions which that treaty involved was formed, without doubt, in consequence of revolutionary agitation, in 1820–21, throughout the Italian peninsula and in parts of Germany. The continental sovereigns then went on with acquisitions and encroachments, mock-charters, and unmeaning constitutions, till Poland was finally sacrificed in 1831; till republican Greece was diplomatized into a kingdom, after barely escaping annexation to Russia; till the Czar Nicholas pushed his dominion to the Pruth; till Hungary was deprived of her franchises; till Italian independent states became "fiefs" of Austria; till the Roman Pope became a puppet of cardinals, controlled by monarchs, and the Turkish Sultan a "sick man," whose will promised the same monarchs a reversion of his estates. Meantime, in 1844, the subtle cabinet of Vienna had taken care to revise its Italian treaties, and pave the way for firmer Austrian foothold in the "boot and spurs" of peninsula possessions. The following treaty of territorial exchange, of new limitation and transfer of reversibility, was concluded at Florence, on the 28th of November, 1844, between Austria, Sardinia, Tuscany, the Duke of Modena, and the Duke of Lucca, crown-Duke of Parma.

"In the name of the most holy and indivisible Trinity, his Royal Highness the Infante of Spain, actual Duke of Lucca and future Duke of Parma, Piacenza and Guastalla; his Royal Highness the Archduke of Austria, Duke of Modena; his Imperial and Royal Highness the Archduke of Austria, Grand Duke of Tuscany—

"Having unanimously recognized that the line of the frontiers of one part of their respective States is complicated, and susceptible of reciprocal ameliorations, easy to be put into operation at the time fixed by the Congress of Vienna, by the different reversions and stipulations; that they cannot remedy the inconveniences of that frontier, except by an exchange at present of small separate portions of their territory; that the power of making these amicable exchanges has been expressly reserved to the parties interested by the 98th article of the act of the Congress of Vienna, but that it cannot be exercised if his Majesty the King of Sardinia and his Imperial Royal and Apostolic Majesty do not consent to a modification of the rights of reversion resulting for them from the treaty of Aix-la-Chapelle of 1748, and from that which was concluded on the 20th of May, 1815, between Austria and Sardinia—rights which are found expressly mentioned in the act of Congress of Vienna, and confirmed by the treaty of Paris of the 10th of June, 1817; the three sovereigns have addressed themselves to this effect to their said Majesties, and his Imperial Royal and Apostolic Majesty recognizes the ability of a better settlement; animated besides by a lively desire to contribute, even at the price of a sacrifice on his part, to a work loudly demanded by the interests of the sovereigns of the said three States, and judging that the best means of attaining that view was to open special negotiations at Florence; and his Majesty the King of Sardinia, being no less desirous of giving to the sovereigns of Lucca, of Modena, and of Tuscany, the greatest proofs of confidence and amity, and having consented to take part in the negotiations, the high contracting Powers have, by their Plenipotentiaries, amicably agreed that the following articles are prescribed in that exchange by the Congress of Vienna:

"Art. I. His Royal Highness the Infante, actual Duke of Lucca, future Duke of Parma, Piacenza and Guastalla, judging it extremely advantageous to annex to his future Duchy of Parma a part of Lunigiana, situated on the southerly slope of the Apennines, and his Imperial and Royal Highness the Grand Duke of Tuscany, deeply desirous of retaining in his possession the two vicariates of Barga and Pietrasanta, which, seeing that they belong to him, are at present separated, and by the reunion of the Duchy of Lucca to Tuscany, stipulated by the 102d article of the Congress of Vienna, will be brought into connection with Tuscany, and ought, consequently, to be ceded, they have agreed to propose to his Royal Highness the Duke of Modena the exchange of the two vicariates of Barga and Pietrasanta for the single Duchy of Guastalla and the Parmesan possessions situated on the right bank of the river Euza. In that case only the Tuscan districts isolated in Lunigiana, and nearest to the Mediterranean, will be ceded to his Royal Highness the future Duke of Parma; and he will obtain thence the only means of exchanging the different boundaries, and of establishing a regular line of frontier with his Royal Highness the Duke of Modena, sole possessor of the equally isolated fiefs in Lunigiana.

"Art. II. His Royal Highness the Duke of Modena, in view of the voluntary offer made to him by his Royal Highness the Infante, actual Duke of Lucca, and future Duke of Parma, of Piacenza and of Guastalla, ' to cede to him, his heirs and successors, in all propriety and sovereignty, the territories situated on the right border of the Euza, with the separate Duchy of Guastalla, at present lying within the bounds of the Lombard and Modenese States, on condition that his Royal Highness the Duke of Modena cedes to him the Modenese territories situate on the left bank of the said river, and that he cedes to Tuscany the two vicariates of Barga and of Pietrasanta, assigned to him by the Congress of Europe,' accepts that exchange, and consequently renounces, for himself, his heirs and successors, the succession of the territories of Bazzano and Scurano, situated on the left bank of the Euza, in favor of his Royal Highness the actual Duke of Lucca. future Duke of Parma, and at the same time renounces claims to the possession of the two vicariates of Barga and of Pietrasanta, assigned to him by the Congress of Vienna, in favor of his Imperial and Royal Highness the Grand Duke of Tuscany, and consents that they shall continue to form in perpetuity, as at present, a part of the Grand Duchy, under the following conditions:

"1. It will be always recognized that he has acquired, in the room of the two vicariates of Pietrasanta and of Barga the formal and absolute possession of the Duchy of Guastalla and of the Parmesian territories on the right bank of the Euza, and he will freely take possession of the territories ceded to him by their legitimate sovereign in lieu of the aforementioned territories of Barga and Pietrasanta.

"2. There will be ceded to him in the vicariate of Barga, the part of the Apennines which extends into the Modenese territory, in such a manner that the frontier shall follow the crest between the mountains of Piastrajo and Porticciola, and not, as at present, on the eastern slope

"The Lake of Porta, situated near the sea, in the vicariat of Pietrasanta, and which is actually divided between the said Tuscan territory and the contiguous Lucchese territory of Montignoso, assigned to him by the Congress of Vienna, remains to him in entirety with the line of territory which is set forth above by article 9th. The Modenese government engages at all times not to permit the cultivation of rice in the district which will be ceded to him, and of preserving the boundaries at present existing, or to substitute any other means whatever to prevent the prejudicial mixing of the salt water with the sweet water ; the Tuscan government engages to leave the water free to run in the lake and in its canal of discharge, the water which it throws out at present, and especially that which comes from Seranezza, and to leave to be taken from Masso di Porto (free from property duties) the materials necessary for the restoration and the preservation of the said boundary, and to authorize the transports by the canal of Porto.

"A practicable route will be opened and sustained, at the expense of Tuscany, through the vicariat of Pietrasanta, from the postal route to the confines of Garfaguana, in the neighborhood of Petrosciana. That route offering the most commodious and the most direct communication between Massa and Garfaguana, will be open in perpetuity to the passage of the Modenese and their merchandise. There will be no exception to this rule, except in extraordinary cases, where the existence of the pest or of cholera-morbus, in the Modenese States shall be proved, and where Tuscany shall establish special hospitals on this point, as upon the other points of the frontier; only in these cases will passage be interdicted to all persons coming from among the Modenese, except they shall have fulfilled in a Tuscan hospital the prescribed quarantine. In other cases of simple suspicion or of an inequality of sanitary measures, passage will be permitted to all persons from the Modenese under a sanitary guard. In the same manner, when the passage of Modenese troops, arms and ammunitions is sought to be made by that route, the Modenese government will give previous notice to the Tuscan government through a ministerial source, except only in the case of an absolute and extraordinary emergence, in which event the previous notification will be given directly by the Governor of Massa or of Garfaguana, to the governmental authority of Pietrasanta. The passage of the objects subjected to duty will be free to the Modenese, but the two governments will agree on a system which will guarantee the Tuscan finances from all loss. His Royal Highness the Duke of Modena, consents that the inhabitants of the vicariats of Barga, and of Pietrasanta, shall profit by the Modenese part of that route of Petrosciana, that might offer to them a more desirable communication for the conveyance of the produce of their lands or for local industry ; the duty which they may pay on their entrance will be entirely restored on their departure from the Modenese States. The execution of this measure will be regulated in the most convenient manner.

"Art. III. His Imperial and Royal Highness the Grand Duke of Tuscany, willing to preserve the two vicariats of Barga and of Pietrasanta annexed to Tuscany, adheres to the above-named conditions, and cedes to his Royal Highness the actual Duke of Lucca and future Duke of Parma, the different possessions scattered in Lunigiana, and, in consequence, he fully consents to every exchange and every new limitation which his Royal Highness might have the intention of contracting with his Royal Highness the Duke of Modena, as much to the advantage of the population of those countries as in the interest of the Ducal possessions, situated to the north of the Apennines.

"Art. IV. His Royal Highness the actual Duke of Lucca, and future Duke of Parma, of Piacenza, and of Guastalla, having the intention, so advantageous to his united duchies of Parma and Piacenza, of acquiring from Tuscany, the districts of Pontremoli, of Bagnone, and those which are dependent in Lunigiana, proper for opening a route to the sea more convenient to commerce, has resolved to renounce his claim to the separate Duchy of Guastalla, and to the districts situate on the right bank of the Euza, in favor of his Royal Highness the Duke of Modena, and consequently cedes for himself, his heirs and successors, all the rights and titles which he has on the right bank of the Euza and on the Duchy of Guastalla. He annexes, on the other hand, to his future Duchy of Parma, not only the territories situated in Lunigiana, which have been ceded to him by Tuscany, and which have not been exchanged with the Duchy of Modena, after the following article, but also the actually Modenese territory on the left bank of the river Euza. He declares that the middle of that river will be considered, from the moment of the reversion contemplated by the 102d article of the Congress of Vienna, as the limits between the States of Parma and Modena, commencing at the point in the Apennines, where it touches the ancient frontier, near the lake Squinico, unto the Po, near Brescello. The navigation which might take place will be always free to the two parties, as well as the use of the watercourses for the removal of the manufactures which are on their borders, free from existing irrigation duties, and without any prejudice to any operations on the opposite shore.

"Art. V. Their Royal Highnesses the Duke of Modena and the present Duke of Lucca and the future Duke of Parma, after having maturely weighed their respective interests in Lunigiana, interrupted at present by the irregular limits which gave place to many political and administrative inconveniences, see that it is impossible to pass by the possessions of the one without frequently and at short distances touching the territory of the other, have resolved to make a division between them of the fiefs and territories now appertaining to the duchy of Modena and to that of Tuscany, in the manner and under the conditions following :

"1. His Royal Highness, the actual Duke of Lucca, future Duke of Parma, having acquired Tuscany in compensation for the cession of the isolated Duchy of Guastalla, and the territories there situated on the Euza, made to his Royal Highness, the Duke of Modena, in Lunigiana, the districts of Pontrenoli, Bagnone, Grappoli, Lusnolo, Terrarossa, Albiano and Calice, amicably exchanged some of his isolated territories for the dispersed fiefs belonging to his Royal Highness the Duke of Modena, and takes in exchange the present separate districts of Treschietto, Villafranca, Castevoli, and Mulazzo into the line of frontier already designated in article ninth, and forms also by the union of those isolated districts one single corps of domain from the southern slope of the Apennines and in immediate contact with the Duchy of Parma by the Cisa.

"2. His Royal Highness, the Duke of Modena, desirous of preserving in his domain in Lunigiana, the most eastern district that of Rochetta, at present separated from the rest of the Modenese and contiguous to the Sardinian States of Aula, on the border of the Magre, takes possession of the district of Calice, to the end of freely attaining it united to the territories which in great part already belong to him, the neighboring districts of Albiano, Pico and Terrarossa, which, conjointly with Calice, will be considered as taking the place of the fiefs of Treschietto, Villafranca, Castevoli and Mulazzo. He renounces those fiefs which the Congress of Vienna—in view of permitting the amicable exchange—has considered as annexed to the States of Massa and Carrara by the different order of succession, and by the rights of reversion preserved in article 98.

"Art. VI. It is agreed by common consent that the exchanged territories will not be burdened with debt, excepting only those which are common to the inhabitants (*communal*), if there be any such debts, and that the other charges which may occur, will remain at the expense of the party ceding. In consequence, the debt (*canon*) which the State of Lucca owes to the commune of Garga for Mount Gragno, will pass from the moment of the reversion to the charge of Tuscany, which is from the present time obliged to cause all the clauses and conditions of ancient copyholds to be declared abrogated and abolished, in such a manner that the Mount de Gragno, now become Tuscan property, shall be free from all cha'ges and responsibility.

"His Royal Highness, the Duke of Modena, will, on all occasions make a special exception in regard to the debt of his future duchy of Guastalla, entered in the registers of the Mount, formerly Napoleon, and consents to provide in lieu and of the Duke of Parma to the payment of the said debt, which, at the time of the reversion, will not be extinguished, according to what the Congress of Vienna, in article 97, as well as successive Commissioners, have fixed at the charge of the legitimate possessor.

"It is also agreed, by common consent, that the edifices, or all other manorial or personal property whatsoever, belonging to the State or to the Crown, will pass with the sovereignty into the different exchanged territories, without causing any loss to the possessors of ecclesiastical property or of pious institutions. It is well understood that free property, if there be any, will remain mutually and reciprocally excepted from these cessions.

"Art. VII. His Majesty, the Emperor of Austria, recognizes the cession of Guastalla and of the territories of the Guza, made to his Royal Highness, the Duke of Modena, by his Royal Highness, the Duke of Lucca, the future Duke of Parma, which he voluntarily renounces, for the reasons developed in this treaty, and guarantees to his Royal Highness, the Duke of Modena, his heirs and successors, that they will not in any manner be disturbed in the peaceable possession of these territories by any persons whatever pretending to the right. He declares himself ready, at the same time, to transfer on the district of Pontremoli and on the rest of that which is assigned in Lunigiana, to the actual Duke of Lucca, the future Duke of Parma, the right of reversion belonging to him upon Guastalla and the territories of the Guza.

"It is agreed between his Majesty the King of Sardinia and his Majesty, the Emperor of Austria, that all the part of Lunigiana which is assigned to the future Duke of Parma, and which comprehends the greatest part of the present Tuscan territories of Pontremoli and Bagnone, as well also as the present Modenese districts of Treschietto, Villafranca, Castevoli and Mulazzo, will be ceded to his Majesty, the King of Sardinia, his heirs and successors, in full propriety and sovereignty, in case the reversion required by the treaty of the 20th of May, 1815, should take place, and that the duchy of Parma will devolve upon Austria, as well as that of Piacenza to Sardinia, and that cession made to Sardinia will form the base of the indemnity; while after the additional and separate article of the above mentioned treaty of the 20th of May, 1815, Austria owes him by agreement to abandon the fortress of Piacenza, with a settled radius, Nevertheless, the value of the aforesaid territories is thus exchanged, namely that of Piacenza, with the settled radius and the Parmesan territories contiguous to the Sardinian States, ought to be established at the same time of the reversion with a spirit of impartiality and of equity by Austrian Sardinian commission; and in case of the slightest difference of opinion it is on both sides agreed to refer the matter to the arbitration of the Holy See.

"Art. IX. This treaty of territorial exchange, of new limitations, and of the transfer of reversibility, will remain secret until the case foreseen in article ninty-nine of the Congress of Vienna, and in the third article of the treaty concluded at Paris on the 10th of June, 1817, is arrived, and at that time it will be immediately put into execution by the courts of Modena, of Parma, and of Tuscany, without any exception, either of act or of right, and with the well-wishing coöperation of two other Powers, which will be done in the following manner :

"His Imperial and Royal Highness, the Archduke and Grand Duke of Tuscany, in taking possession of the Duchy of Lucca, assigned to him by the 102 article of the act of Vienna, retains the two vicalrates of Barga and Pietrasanta contiguous to that duchy. There is in separation only the part of the Apennines which, between the abrupt mounts of Prastrajo and Porticciola, discharge their waters into the Modenese territories, which are opposite, and to which it will belong in the future ; a line of limitation will be fixed by common consent, by the Modenese and Tuscan commissioners, which, following exactly the crest between the two slopes, commences and ends at the spot where the two lines descend from the Modenese slope, in such a manner that, in abandoning them, they will draw an entirely new line of about 22,000 fathoms from Vienna, which would unite the actual confines in Porticciola to those which, in descending from Mount Plastrajo, form the limit of the territory of Barga toward the Modenese Garfaguana. That limit, extending to the limit of Serchio, between Castelvecchio, and Fiattone, follows the river unto Torrite-Pava, which in future will separate the Tuscan territory—now the Duchy of Lucca—from the Lucchese district of Gallicano, which will pass to his Royal Highness the Duke of Modena. Thence, following the ancient sinuous frontier, it will be directed a little above Campolescini to the vicariat of Pietrasanta, of which the frontier rests where it actually stands in regard to the Duchy of Modena, unto the locality where, on Mount Carchio, it touches the present Lucchese district of Montenoso ; thence, following the eastern line which separates it from the vicariate of Pietrasanta, it will continue until it approaches the lake of Porta. And as it is said in article 2, section 3, that a fixed radius will be accorded around that lake, which becomes Modenese, the frontier will be traced in concert with the Tuscan and Modenese commissioners in a manner fixed from the present time, as follows : At the distance of 400 fathoms (braccia) Tuscan measurement, on the shore setting out from the mouth of the canal of the Lake of Porta, there will be marked a line of 1,500 braccia, following the direction of the path which leads to a house marked No. 16, in the chart of the Tuscan rental; a second line of 265 braccia turning on the path to the right, will be drawn from the extreme point of that line ; then a third line of 1,360 braccia, to reach the canal of Seranezza at the distance of 100 braccia from the discharging canal of the lake; thence, following the eastern side of the said route of the Casetta for a length of 1,400 braccia, it will close the figure by a last line of 1,700 braccia to the actual limits of Montenoso at the distance of 400 braccia from the postal route. It is understood that in the circumference will be comprised, and by that is ceded to his Royal Highness the Duke of Modena, the maritime fortress of Cinguale, and the corps de garde, the sluices, the house above mentioned, and the route which leads to it.

"His Royal Highness the Archduke, Duke of Modena, will take possession of the territories assigned to him by the Congress of Vienna and not ceded by the present treaties, that is to say of the Lucchese territory of Montenoso, Minucciana, Castiglione and Gallicano, as well as that of Fivizzano, actually Tuscan. On one side it will be free from all obligation contracted by the Convention of the 4th of March, 1819, with the Court of Lucca concerning Castiglione; on the other side it will be held to indemnify Tuscany for the capital which she has employed in the construction of the military route of Fivizzano, in conformity with the act of the 5th November, 1829 ; on the arrival of the Tuscan Commissioners, it will immediately take possession of the territory of Barga already specified on the Modenese line of the Apennines, and of which it is situated about the Lake of Porta already described, and which is near the western extremity of the Tuscan territory, of Pietrasanta, as well as in Lunigiana of the Tuscan districts of Albiano, Calice, Rico and Terrarossa, conserving exactly the actual frontier toward the Piedmontese, and following the new Parmesan State in Lunigiana, the boundaries in great part formerly described as hereafter, which are colored on the accompanying map, to wit: The actual limit which separates the Modenese district of Rochetta from that actually Tuscan one of Pontremoli in an extent of 1,800 fathoms from Vienna, and the winding limit which separates the Tuscan district of Calice from the Modenese district of Mulazzo, between Casoni and Parana, in an extent of 3,070 ulterior fathoms, will be simply united to Casoni by the shorter line of the new limitation, 200 fathoms long; from the one new line of 2,540 fathoms, between Parana and the point nearest to the frontier of Lusuolo, above Castevoli, following from the first the road of Tresana, on the Mount Coletta, then descending to the left in the river of Conosilla. On leaving this point it will follow the said frontier of Lusuolo unto the other point on the Magra, distant 2,780 fathoms; thence it will be directed between Farnoli and Terrarossa, setting out from la Magra unto the river Civiglia, a new and last direct line of 700 fathoms, through the route of Pontremoli to a distance of 300 fathoms above Piastra; thence will come the ancient limit which ascends the Apennines for a length of 8,770 fathoms, separating the Modenese district of Lucciana, and of Varano on the Tanerone, which remains, as well as Firigano to the Duchy of Modena, from Bagnonals, which is Tuscan at present, but which ought to become Parmesan; also the curved line of frontier between the Duchies of Modena, and Parma, in Lunigiana, in which they extend for a length of 19,360 fathoms from one summit of the mountains to the other, which inclose the river of Magra, will be 15,920 fathoms of ancient limit, and only 3,440 of new limit, already indicated, and which is simply divided into three lines easy to trace—the first of 200 fathoms, the second of 2,540, the third of 700, in the precise direction of west to east.

" His Royal Highness the actual Duke of Lucca, and future Duke of Parma, will not take the government and the title of the Duchy of Guastalla, to which he renounces all claim, nor those of the territory on the right bank of the Euza, which he also renounces in favor of His Royal Highness the Duke of Modena; but he will make to that sovereign, by the Parmesan commissaries named for that purpose, the immediate cession of the one and the other of those territories, as well as the territories in Lunigiana, in the manner before indicated in section 4. At the same time, his Royal Highness the Duke of Modena will make to him, by the Modenese Commissioners, the cession of the territories of Treschietto, Villafranca, Castevoli and Mulazzo, in Lunigiana, according to the line of frontier before indicated, in the same manner as the districts situated on the left bank of the Euza. Also that river which descends from Mount Giogo de Fivizanno, and cuts near the lake Squinico, in the Apennines, the frontier preserved through three miles of Italy, between the Duchies of Modena and Parma, on the Mounts Tendola and Malpasso, which will serve in the future for a limit between the two States, from that lake to the Po; and while the Duchy of Modena thus acquires from the superior regions the territory of Succiso, between the Euza and the actual boundary, it renounces that of Scurano, which follows immediately on the left bank, and finally acquires on the right bank the district of Ciano, and in the plain those of Gattatico, Poviglio and San Giorgio unto the embouchure of that river in the Po above Brescello, to make no more than one single body of domain, with Guastalla, between the Po and the Mediterranean. The Duchy of Guastalla, of which his Royal Highness the Duke of Modena, after the cessions made to him, takes the sovereignty and the title, preserves toward the Lombardo-Venetian kingdom the same limits which separate him at present from the said kingdom. On the other side, his Royal Highness the actual Duke of Lucca, future Duke of Parma, in taking, conformably with article 99th and 102d of the treaty of Vienna, the sovereign government of his new State, and in making without delay the cession agreed to, will also take, in common concord with the sovereigns of Modena and Parma, the most prompt measures for the new limitation, after the rules above laid down in the plan, so that all incertitude or discussion may be avoided in the important moment of the transfer of so much territory to new sovereigns, and the changing of the ancient lines of complicated frontiers into new and better regulated lines after the nature of the places and reciprocal territorial and commercial convenience. He will assume, in concert with the Modenese Commissioners named for that purpose, with as little delay as possible, his immediate domain on Bazzano and Scurano, on the left bank of the Euza, and on Treschietto, Villafranca, Castevoli and Mulazzo, appertaining to the duchy of Modena, as well as that on Pontremoli, Bagnone, Merizzo, Fornoli, Groppoli and Lusuelo, belonging to Tuscany; that he will deliver immediately to the name of his Royal Highness the Duke of Modena, the territories of Albiano, Calice, Rico, and Terrarossa, already ceded to him. It is understood that from the present time the reversion of the imposts will be received on behalf of the sovereign to whom the territory will devolve by the present treaty, free from the arrears which will rest on the party ceding the territory.

" Art. X. The present treaty, drawn up in fivefold form, with the chart attached, will be signed, as that chart, by the respective plenipotentiaries, who will thereto attach their arms and seals. It will be ratified, and the ratifications exchanged at Florence within the space of two months, or earlier if possible.

" Done at Florence, on the 28th of the month of November, in the year of grace 1844

" CARREGA.   G. FORNI.
CAV. VACANI DI FORT 'OLIVO.   H. CORSINI."
A. FAFAELLI.

The above treaty of Florence, being of a nature, in many of its stipulations, to invite comment, and perhaps provoke opposition on the part of other powers, the following further separate and secret article was subsequently agreed upon by the high contracting powers, to be reverted to in case of need:

" SEPARATE SECRET ARTICLE OF THE TREATY OF FLORENCE.

" The contracting sovereigns are agreed that if, contrary to all probability, there should arise any opposition from any one power whatsoever, and that they or their successors, through causes inherent to those territories, and preëxistent to the present treaty, cannot enter into, or might be disturbed in the peaceable possession of the territories—all the stipulations which have to-day been made by virtue of their sovereign rights after the sense of the act of the Congress of Vienna, will be regarded as null and void, and consequently all the dispositions of the act of the Congress of Vienna will remain intact, or be reëstablished, so that the Duchy of Guastalla and the other Parmesan territories mentioned in the treaty will remain to the sovereign of Parma; that his royal highness the Duke of Modena, will take possession of Pietrasanta and Barga, and that his imperial and royal highness the Grand Duke of Tuscany, will keep the vicariates of Pontremoli and Bagnone.

" The present separate and secret article will have the same force and value as if it were inserted, word for word, in the treaty of this day. It will be ratified and the ratifications exchanged at the same time.

" In witness whereof, the respective plenipotentiaries have affixed their seals and arms.

" Done at Florence, the 23th of the month of November, in the year of grace, 1844.

" CARREGA.   G. FORNI.
CAV. VACANI DI FORT 'OLIVO.   H. CORSINI."
A. RAFAELLI.

IV.

Satisfactory advances having been made, by the Florence negotiations, toward further Austro-Italian possession, the grand object of military occupation, by Austrian troops, was gained, at a later period, through the subjoined treaty of alliance, offensive and defensive, between the Emperor of Austria and the Duke of Modena, signed at Vienna, December 24th, 1847.

"TREATY BETWEEN AUSTRIA AND MODENA.

"His majesty the Emperor of Austria and his royal highness the archduke, Duke of Modena, animated by a reciprocal desire of advantageously uniting again the bonds of friendship and relationship which exist between them, and to watch by their common efforts for the maintenance of interior peace and of legal order in their States, have agreed in this respect to a special treaty.

"Art. 1. In all cases where the Italian States of his majesty the Emperor of Austria and of his royal highness the Duke of Modena might be exposed to an attack from without, the high contracting parties reciprocally engage themselves to lend aid and assistance, by all means in their power, according to the demands that may be made by one of the two parties to the other.

"Art. 2. As the States of his royal highness the Duke of Modena enter into the line of defence of the Italian provinces of his majesty the Emperor of Austria, his royal highness the Duke of Modena accords to his majesty the Emperor of Austria the right of advancing his imperial troops on the Modenese territory, and to occupy all the fortified places during such time as the interest of the common defence or military prudence might demand.

"Art. 3. Should occurrences take place in the interior of the States of his royal highness the Duke of Modena, of a nature to cause it to be feared that order and tranquillity might be disturbed, or if the tumultuous movements of the people should extend to the proportions of a veritable insurrection, for the repression of which the means at the disposal of the government may not be sufficient, his majesty the Emperor of Austria engages, as soon as a demand shall have been made upon him, to lend all the military assistance necessary for the maintenance or reëstablishment of tranquillity and lawful order.

"Art. 4. His royal highness the Duke of Modena engages not to celebrate with any other power any military convention whatever without the previous consent of his imperial and royal apostolic majesty.

"Art. 5. A special convention will immediately regulate everything relating to the expenses and maintenance of the troops of one of the two parties which may operate on the territory of the other.

"Art. 6. The present treaty will be ratified, and the ratifications will be exchanged in the space of fifteen days, or earlier if possible.

"In witness of which we, the plenipotentiaries of his majesty the Emperor of Austria and of his royal highness the Duke of Modena, have signed the present convention, and affixed their seals thereto.

PRINCE DE METTERNICH,
COUNT THEODORE DE VOLO."

Intent on these and similar constant approaches toward a centralizing system in Italy, such as aggregates her Sclavonic possessions, Austria has neglected no opportunity (spite of Vienna treaties of 1815) to consolidate her dominion in the Italian peninsula. The diplomatic distrust growing out of these secret treaties has aroused the watchful jealousy of Louis Napoleon, and given him a long-sought opportunity, with apparent reason on his side, to demand a definite withdrawal of Austrian influence from independent Italy. The abrogation of secret treaties between the Court of Vienna and Italian princes, has been strenuously insisted upon by the French, and as steadily resisted by the Austrian emperor. There is little doubt that a much feebler provocation than treaties like the above would have sufficed for an occasion of war at the present time. "The hour and the man" provide the genuine *casus belli ;* and until a wrestle and a fall shall proclaim one less dynasty on the continent, we may look for rapidly-changing scenes in the old, oft-rehearsed tragedy of European war.

V.

It is probable that ulterior and carefully concealed motives urge on the three heads of belligerent nations thus far actively involved. The French banner of Italian Nationality may have a reverse legend equivalent to Italian annexation, whilst the Black Eagles of Hapsburg may behold an ultimate quarry in the whole of Italy, from Alps to ocean. . . . . Between both, stands Victor Emanuel, perhaps calculating the chance of a wide national sovereignty, perhaps reliant upon Napoleon III. alone ! . . . . But behind all, Revolution may be watching the turn of events, and awaiting the moment when it can sweep from the Seven Hills of Rome, and bear back the armies of Austria and France.

VI.

The direct provocation to present hostilities between Austria and France, may be traced to the close relations of the court of Vienna with the petty potentates of Italy. Its private conventions and treaties with Tuscans, Lucchese, Modenese, and Papal States, were so many steps of advance into the heart of southern Italy. On the other hand, Austria and Sardinia had ground for jealous watchfulness of each other; since it was Sardinia that, in 1848, under Charles Albert, raised the standard of Italian Nationality, and in 1849 succumbed only to superior force at the battle of Novara. Since 1848, Austria has beheld in the Piedmontese capital a focus of revolutionary feeling, and in Charles Albert's son, the present Sardinian king, an ambitious and dangerous neighbor to Lombardy and Venice. The policy constrained upon Austria, by her political structure, is an unfortunate one, because it admits of no relaxation of military rule over subject provinces. Hence the Ticino River has demarked on the east an Italian state held by foreign conquest, and its natives oppressed by alien soldiers, while on the west the same stream bordered another Italian state comparatively free, possessed by her children, and independent of foreign influence. The contrast has been constantly favorable to Victor Emanuel's government, till patriots throughout the peninsula, republicans not excepted, have become accustomed to regard " Constitutional Sardinia," as the hope of reconstructed Italy. Whether Victor Emanuel be capable of emulating Washington, in the event of entire Italian enfranchisement, or whether he will be only desirous of enlarging his own dynastic empire, are questions that the future must answer ; but that he is successful in drawing around him the national sympathies of his countrymen, needs no better proof than the fact that republican Garibaldi supports him with all the prestige of democratic antecedents.

VII.

Against such a revolutionary neighbor as Sardinia, the Austrian government conceived it necessary to strengthen its Italian dominion ; and hence the secret treaties, whereby important military positions and the right of occupation or passage by Austrian troops, were granted from Tuscany, Parma, Guastalla, Modena, and Pontifical states. These encroachments on territories whose permanent independence was guaranteed by the Congress of Vienna, may have been thought necessary to the preservation of " legitimate " Austrian sovereignty, or they may herald ulterior objects embracing the absorption of Papal territory, and the control of Naples. Whatever designs of conquest were concealed, however, is of no material interest now, since the Sardinian monarch, backed by France, has assumed the championship of Italy ; but it is manifest that grounds existed, in the secret treaties alone, to warrant an interference of a state so menaced as Piedmont was by an unscrupulous neighbor. Her representations, through Count Cavour, may have influenced Napoleon III. to interfere actively, but there is little doubt that the French emperor has his own motives for his own course. Great Britain sought to mediate between the Courts of Turin and Vienna, some months before hostilities commenced. Lord Cowley, as her representative, repaired to Paris, to be received confidentially by Napoleon, and cleverly referred to the Emperor of Austria. The British ambassador then went to Vienna, was cordially received by Francis Joseph, and sent home with assurances that all difficulties would be settled. The Emperor of Russia then proposed that a grand Congress of the Five Powers, Austria, Russia, Great Britain, France, and Prussia, should be convened to settle the Affairs of Empire. Napoleon was quite disposed to this project, because he felt that France would have the leading voice in such a congress; but Great Britain became apprehensive that it would open discussions on general continental affairs, and perhaps involve her own occupation of strongholds like Malta and Gibraltar. She stipulated, therefore, that if a congress should be called, its action must be confined to the adjustment of the Italian imbroglio arising out of treaties between Austria and her ducal allies. Austria, likewise, refused to assent to the proposed assembling of a congress except on condition that Sardinia should disarm, and France recall her warlike preparations. The demands of Great Britain and Austria were discussed for some time, and at last agreed upon as the basis of a congress; and it was decided that commissioners should be at once appointed to arrange for a mutual disarmament. It was at this juncture that Austria concluded to take another step, withdrawing relations with the court of Turin, and precipitating war upon Sardinian frontiers. Such is a brief *résumé* of the immediate antecedents of this war.

VIII.

What ultimate reorganization of European politics may date from the results of present strife must yet remain veiled to all but speculative vision. That the traditional Balance of Power, which has been the pretended aim of so many struggles in the past is not to be founded on dynastic assumptions, will be proved by this as by former wars. . . . . Italy cannot be dominated by monarchs without infidelity to her highest historical truths. Her self-sustaining resources, her commercial facilities, her mountain chains, are all linked with recollections of freedom; and to be permanently great, she must be permanently republican. . . . . Bounded by a free Italian Confederation, the Free Cantons of Switzerland might smile at Austrian encroachment. Bavaria and Saxony, with representative governments, and the Hanse Towns, strengthened by renewed liberalism, could balance monarchism in Central Europe. Austria, with Catholic Bohemia, Prussia, with her Protestant States, would not then combine against popular governments, but must rely upon their aid, to keep back the Colossus of the North. The Scandinavian peninsula might balance Russia on the Baltic by a confederacy with Denmark and the States of Holland. Such a reconstruction of continental sovereignties, with Hungary and Poland revived into constitutional nationalities, and Greece once more a popular commonwealth, would present a balance of power worthy to be maintained, and open for Europe—so long chained to wheels of dynastic chariots—a Future worthy to measure itself with that of our own Republic of the West. Sclavonic races, whether now controlled by Turkey or Austria, must gravitate toward Russia by natural laws. Scandinavia, true to her extraction, will be true to national independence. Wherever the German tongue is spoken, there must Germans confederate; while Saxon and Celt, Italian and Iberian remain, from their instincts, separate and independent. By old world aggregation of nationalities, the designs of nature must be, as they have ever been, developed to their proper term; whilst in our own magnificent world the problem of progressive homogeneity shall in good time be unravelled beneath the eye of God.

BIOGRAPHICAL SKETCHES, ARMIES, AND FINANCES.

I.

CAMILLI DI CAVOUR was born in Turin, July 14th, 1809. His father was a merchant, engaged in extensive commercial transactions, whereby he amassed a considerable fortune, which he bequeathed to the subject of this sketch. Camilli became first popularly known through his connection with *Il Risorgimento*, an Italian liberal journal established in 1847. His vigorous articles upon political economy in that paper attracted much attention, and in 1849 he was returned through liberal influences to the Sardinian Chamber of Deputies. He recommended himself by his conservative course, as a deputy, and in the course of two following years received, from the Court of Turin, an appointment, firstly, as Minister of Agriculture, and then, in addition, the portfolio of Minister of Finance. . . . . His career in public employment and royal favor was subsequently quite rapid. In 1852 he was made President of the Council of State, after having been ennobled, with title of Count, by the king. As minister for Foreign Affairs, he opposed the pope's concessions to Austrian policy, and was instrumental in effecting an alliance of Sardinia with France, Great Britain, and Turkey, in the war against Russia. At the termination of difficulties, he attended the Peace Conference of Paris, as special representative of Sardinia, and took an active part in urging a general movement toward reform in Italian affairs. He protested against the occupation of Papal States by foreign troops, and sought to induce an interference with the government of Naples, to the extent of ameliorating the rigorous home policy of Ferdinand. As minister of State in Sardinia, he carried through several measures for suppressing convents and monasteries, and bringing their property under civil control. For this course of action, he was excommunicated by the pope, and met with bitter opposition from the clergy, but was sustained by the general feeling of the nation. . . . . Count Cavour has always shown himself a strong partisan of France, and in 1858, after the attempt to assassinate Louis Napoleon at Paris, January 14th, he submitted a law providing for the arrest and extradition of any conspirators against the life of foreign princes who might seek refuge in Sardinian territory, but allowing the trial of such persons, on appeal, by a jury of two hundred, named by municipal authorities. This measure was unpopular with the people, and Cavour was accused of being too zealous a friend of the French emperor. There is no doubt that a very good understanding exists between Napoleon III. and the Sardinian minister, whether it be the result of policy or not ; and Count Cavour has earned the confidence of his imperial friend by a steady adherence to French interests, as opposed to Austria in all questions that have grown out of the war of 1854, in reference to the Danubian Principalities. Whether he may be disposed to act the part of the Prince of Peace, or whether he shall prove himself, in the end, a staunch nationalist—*nous verrons*. Count Cavour is now at the head of Civil Affairs in Sardinia, and chief confidant of the allied monarchs.

II.

FRANCOIS CERTAIN DE CANROBERT is a native of Brittany, France, where he was born in 1809, and is, therefore, of the same age as Count Cavour. In 1826, he was a member of the Military School of St. Cyr, but afterward entered the French army as a private soldier, and subsequently rose to be a sub-lieutenant. In 1835, he went to Africa, received a commission as first lieutenant in the expedition of Mascara, and was promoted to a captaincy before 1837. He distinguished himself at the assault on Constantine, winning his medal of the Legion of Honor. Being now in active African service, his rise was certain. He became a major in 1842, lieutenant-colonel in 1846, and brigadier-general in 1849. Returning to France, he was made aide-de-camp to Napoleon, and supported the Prince-President in his memorable *coup d'état*, after which he was dispatched to the provinces with authority as military commissioner, to suppress all resistance to the new order of things. In 1853, Canrobert was made general of division, and in the year following accompanied a French army to the Crimea, where he speedily displayed himself, and was wounded in the battle of Alma. On a vacancy in the supreme command, Canrobert, pursuant to secret instructions from the emperor, took the place of general-in-chief St. Arnaud. He defeated the Russians at Inkermann, and afterward resigned his position, as commander, in favor of General Pelissier. At the close of the ensuing campaign, he returned to France, high in favor with Napoleon, and was soon after accredited minister to Sweden. He is now a Marshal of France, and was in command of one of the great military departments, till summoned at the commencement of present hostilities between the French and Austrian governments, to take post in the army of Italy under Napoleon himself.

III.

Giuseppe Garibaldi was born at Nice, on the borders of Genoa, on the 4th of July, 1807. Like his countryman Columbus, he belonged to a sea-faring family, and though educated for the priesthood, found himself in early manhood treading the decks of a merchant vessel. In common with many Italian patriots, he mourned over the degradation of his country under foreign rule, and when the secret organization of "Young Italy" began to develop its projects, the youthful mariner hastened to enroll himself in the ranks of Italy's defenders. The abortive attempt at revolution in 1834 brought Garibaldi under ban of the Piedmontese government, and he was hunted for a fortnight, through the mountains, ere he could effect his escape over the French border. Charles Albert, father of the present King of Sardinia, proclaimed him a rebel under sentence of death ; but he continued to follow his profession as a sailor, under the French flag, till he found an opportunity of aiding another free cause by enlisting in the service of the Montevidean Republic, then struggling against Rosas, the dictator of Buenos Ayres. He was made commodore of the Montevidean fleet, which he manned with European refugees, most of whom were members of the society of "Young Italy." He married a Montevidean lady, and distinguished himself as a skillful strategist and commander, both on sea and land, materially contributing to the successful resistance of Montevideo against Rosas, till the current of events in Italy began setting toward another revolutionary struggle, which manifested itself in the outbreaks of 1848 . . . . . In the spring of that year, Garibaldi, with a force of Italian compatriots, left South America and landed at Nice, where the people were already in arms against the Austrians. The patriots flocked around him, and he soon found himself at the head of a formidable legion, with which he hastened to offer his services to Charles Albert, the sovereign who had condemned him to death fifteen years before, but who had now declared himself the constitutional protector of Italy, in her efforts for emancipation. The Sardinian king was constrained to accept his revolutionary subject's offer of assistance, but he allowed him no opportunity to engage in actual service. Garibaldi, and his republican followers, numbering nearly four thousand men, were kept in the background till the defeat of Victor-Emanuel at the battle of Novarra, and his subsequent abandonment of the Italian cause, left the country without a leader, and at the mercy of Radetzky, the Austrian general, and Ferdinand the tyrant of Naples. . . . In this crisis the democratic chief divided his forces, in which were Jacopo Medici, Joseph Mazzini, and Gavazzi, by sea and land, and succeeded in throwing himself into Rome about the time that Pius IX. fled from that city, to take refuge at Gaeta. When a republic was subsequently declared by the Roman revolutionists, Garibaldi was associated with Mazzini and Avezzano, in a Triumvirate government. . . . . Soon afterward, in response to the pope's appeal, an army of French, Austrians, Spanish, and Neapolitans, laid siege to Rome, which was gallantly defended by the republicans until a capitulation was forced by the bombardment of the city. Garibaldi and his legion made head to the last, and evacuated the city with arms in their hands, and without disbandment. Their leader, in announcing his determination to depart, addressed the following proclamation to his companions :

" Soldiers, what I have to offer is fatigue, danger, struggling and death—the chill of the cold night, the open air, and the burning sun ; no lodgings, no munitions, no provisions—but forced marches, dangerous watchposts, and continual struggling with bayonets against batteries. Let those who love freedom and their country better than their life follow me."

Four thousand brave men responded to this appeal, and with this force, Garibaldi hoped to fight his way to Venice, which still held nobly out against the Austrians. Gaining possession of several small vessels and boats, he embarked upon the Adriatic, but before reaching the lagunes, was attacked by an Austrian squadron, and forced to regain the shore. The Austrians followed up the success by land pursuit, causing a dispersion of the republicans. Garibaldi, on whose head a heavy price was set, escaped to the mountains, with a few faithful comrades, and his South American wife, who had been a sharer in all his toils and dangers. On the eve of becoming a mother, this generous woman refused to seek some friendly shelter, but insisted on accompanying her husband in his flight toward Ravenna. She was carried sometimes on a litter by the soldiers, sometimes in Garibaldi's arms, over precipices and through a wilderness country, the Austrians pressing close behind, till they entered the heart of the mountains. But the poor lady's strength failed under fatigue and exposure, till on reaching a goatherd's lonely hut, Garibaldi asked for shelter, and bore his fainting wife to a rude pallet of straw, laid upon planks. As he laid her there, unclasping her hands from his neck, she unclosed her eyes, smiled faintly, and sunk to eternal sleep, at the moment when an alarm outside announced the approach of pursuers. Garibaldi, paralyzed by the loss of his beloved Aneeta, felt almost inclined to abandon the effort to escape ; but his faithful followers hurried him from the spot, so soon as the remains of his wife had been committed to a hasty grave. The goatherd, whose cabin afforded this brief shelter, was soon after seized and murdered by the Austrians, while the corpse of Garibaldi's wife was subjected to their barbarous insults. The republican chief himself, wandered for more than a month through Apennine wildernesses, until, venturing into Piedmont, he was arrested by the Sardinian authorities. Subsequently released, he sailed for the United States, where he remained till 1854, engaged in peaceful, laborious pursuits. When the Sardinian government, influenced by the prudence of Count Cavour, adopted the liberal policy which has distinguished it throughout several years

past, Garibaldi was invited to establish himself at Genoa. Associating himself with mercantile affairs, he apparently withdrew from political agitation,
and during two years resided on a small family estate, where the present summons to national Italy, found him ready to renew the strife for independence.
It is a matter of doubt whether Victor Emanuel is less averse to the republican chieftain's active coöperation than was his father, Charles Albert ; but
the astute Cavour and his patron, Napoleon III. are aware that Garibaldi's
name is a host in itself, and that to refuse a command to him would be to cast
suspicion upon the purity of the alleged motives that call France to the assistance of Italy.   Garibaldi embodies in his command the democratic soldiery of
Italy ; and his career will be watched, not only by his countrymen and their
king, but quite as anxiously by the real well-wishers of Italy, in every quarter
of the world.

IV.

FIELD-MARSHAL, OR FELDZEUGMEISTER GYULAI, is a Magyar by nationality,
born at Pesth, in 1798. His father distinguished himself in the Austrian
army, by effective service, at the battle of Aspern, fought in 1809, between
Napoleon I. and the Archduke Charles. Young Gyulai's advent in military life was during the last campaigns conducted by Austria and her allies,
against the declining power of Bonaparte. He served as an under lieutenant in
a regiment commanded by his father, comprising the Gyulai and Lichtenstein
huzzars ; and in 1827, was commissioned as major in the emperor's Hulan
corps. After passing through the grade of infantry colonel, he was created a
general in 1837, and stationed at Vienna, in the imperial guard. In 1846, he was
transferred to the Dalmatian frontier, with the title of Field-marshal-lieutenant,
and military supervision over the provincial circle, of which Trieste is the
centre. He held this post at the period of revolutionary excitement in 1848,
when Italy to the Tyrol, and Germany to the gates of Vienna, threatened to
throw cff Austrian domination. Faithful to his family loyalty, Gyulai took
prompt measures to place the sea-board from Fiume to Trieste in a state of
defence against a threatened descent from the Italian peninsula. He assumed
dictatorial powers, dismissed from service, or transferred to the interior, all
officers suspected of revolutionary tendencies, reorganized the land forces and
sea armament, and by his vigilance preserved Dalmatia from the consequences
of an unforeseen attack by Sardinian men-of-war, sent out to reduce Trieste.
His devotion and marked ability, as a commander, placed Gyulai high in favor
with the emperor, who bestowed upon him several decorations and titles.
In 1849, he was made Minister of War, and is said to have planned the campaign which resulted in the overthrow of Hungarian Revolutionists. After
the repression of disturbances, Gyulai traversed the whole empire as military
inspector, and drew up an elaborate report of the condition of the provinces ;
soon after which he withdrew from the War Department, and was transferred to
the Lombardo-Venetian kingdom, with the rank of *Feldzeugmeister*, and the order
of the Golden Fleece. General Radetzky then held chief command over the
provinces that he had subdued in 1849 ; but at his subsequent retirement,
Gyulai became general of the Austro-Italian army, which he now commands.
By special appointment of the emperor, at the beginning of the war, he is also
viceroy of the Lombardo-Venetian kingdom, in place of the Archduke Maximilian, recalled to Vienna by his imperial brother Francis Joseph. The present is Gyulai's first campaign as commander-in-chief, though he has seen service before.

V.

The death of Ferdinand II., King of the Two Sicilies, at the critical period of an Italian war, renders the position of his successor a subject of interest. The wretched tyrant who has just passed from earth—after undergoing in his own person, a succession of living deaths, that seemed avenging inflictions for his manifold crimes—was a true Bourbon, headstrong, double-dealing, cruel and fanatical. The bombardment of his own capital—an act which he commanded, in order to repress a patriotic manifestation—attached to him while living, the sobriquet of " King Bomba ;" but now that he is dead, there is little need of further animadversion on his life, save that embraced in the above-made assertion, that he was a true Bourbon. His queen belonged to the House of Austria. A daughter of the Archduke Charles, she inherited the sternness and duplicity of the Hapsburgs, and was a fitting consort of her Neapolitan spouse in his bigotry, though far excelling him in administrative ability. During Ferdinand's life she headed the Austrian party of Naples, and labored to secure the succession for her eldest son, Count De Trani, in opposition to the prior claims of the Prince-Royal Francis, Duke of Calabria, a son of the king by his first wife, Maria, who was a daughter of Victor Emanuel VI., brother of Charles Albert and uncle of the present King of Sardinia. . . . . The late Ferdinand of Naples was greatly under the influence of his Austrian consort, Maria Theresa, and it was feared he would name her favorite as his successor; but the legitimate heir is now recognized, in FRANCIS II. The new monarch, as before said, is a relative of the Sardinian King, being the son of Victor Emanuel's cousin Marie. He is in his twenty-third year, his step-brother, Count de Trani, being twenty-one. Francis II. was lately married to a Bavarian princess, whose family relations are bound up with Austrian policy; and he himself is reported to be under control of the priests. But there is a strong Sardinian party in Naples, which maintains that the young king is at heart disposed to throw off the yoke of priestly and foreign influence. The crisis of Italian transition, now once more approaching, will determine whether the successor of Ferdinand shall disarm revolution by placing himself on Victor Emanuel's platform of nationality, or whether he will take arms to oppose a Muratist movement that appears to be threatened by the progress of French intervention.

VI.

The retirement, or dismissal, of Count Buol Schaunstein, late Austrian foreign minister, from his position in the Imperial Council, gives rise for apprehension that the Hapsburg policy is reverting to the character which it maintained under Metternich and Schwartzenburg—of dogged adherence to the traditions of despotic rule. Count Buol, whatever might have been his faults of omission—was at least a statesman of common-sense proclivities ; and it is not to be doubted that he deplored and would have averted, if possible, the war entailed upon his government. His removal, and the appointment of Count Rechberg in his place, is suggestive, at this time, of a determination on the part of his imperial master to push the quarrel with France to extremities. Count JOHN BERNARD RECHBERG is a Bavarian, born October 14, 1806, on the same day that Austria lost the double battle of Auerstadt and Jena. His father was Count Albert Francis of Rechberg, one of the numberless petty chiefs who claimed feudal sovereignty before the era of the French revolution ; but as John was a younger son, he entered, after leaving the university, into Austrian military service. In 1841, having attained the rank of colonel

Rechberg left the army for a diplomatic career. He was intrusted by Prince Metternich with several confidential missions, and went to the court of St. Petersburg as secretary of legation ; but in the troubles of 1848–9, he reëntered the army, and distinguished himself by opposition to revolutionary ideas. When "order reigned" once more, Rechberg was rewarded for his loyalty with a place in the cabinet, under the Prime Minister, Prince Schwartzenberg. He was employed in the negotiations of Olmutz, and became a favorite of the emperor, and Archduchess Sophia. In 1855, he represented Austria in the Frankfort Diet, presiding over the independent States, and neutralizing Prussian influence by his skillful political tactics. Count Rechberg is a man of energy and a thorough-going advocate of "dynastic legitimacy." He is a pupil of Metternich and Schwartzenberg, in their absolutist dogmas, and as unscrupulous in the means necessary to uphold them. Arbitrary and uncompromising, he is not the man to offer or accept terms from Napoleon III. that are not based on entire recognition of Austrian claims. He is likewise popular in Germany, and being a Bavarian, may exert due influence through his position, on the new king of Naples, whose queen is a Bavarian princess.—Altogether, with Count Rechberg, Austria becomes bolder and craftier, if not wiser in maintaining dynastic claims.

VII.

BARON DE HESS, next in command to Count Gyulai, in the Austro-Italian army, was born in the year 1788. He has seen nearly half a century of service, and has been attached to the Austrian army in Italy since 1829–30, during which period, as well as in the revolutionary seasons of 1848–49, he distinguished himself on many occasions. He was chief of Gen. Radetzky's staff in the campaigns against the Sardinians, under Charles Albert, and was much trusted by the Austrian commander-in-chief, both as a soldier and counsellor. It is said that he opposed the plan of Count Gyulai in reference to crossing the Ticino at the outset of the war, and it is not improbable that, on the score of greater military experience and ability, he may yet supersede the Feldzeugmeister in command of the Austrian van. . . . . . . General HEBEL, another Austrian commander, likewise served under Radetzky, in 1848, being intrusted with a division of occupation between Verona and Trent, along the line of the Adige River. He was with the Imperial Chasseurs in an engagement near Pastrengo, where the Austrians sustained a defeat, and was in command at the time several Italian prisoners were shot in a ditch at Trent.

VIII.

Marshal BARAGUAY D'HILLIERS was born in 1796. He has been noted in past years as a partisan of strong government in France, and was at one time proposed by the opponents of liberalism as the fitting leader of a reactionary movement against the revolution of 1848. After the reduction of Rome, and retreat of Garibaldi, in 1849, General d'Hilliers was sent to Italy, and succeeded Gen. Oudinot in command of the army of occupation in the Papal States. At the period when Louis Napoleon contemplated his famous *coup d'état*, Marshal d'Hilliers was selected as a trusty instrument to be used against the republic, and he was placed in command of the Parisian troops, displacing Changarnier, Cavaignac, and other generals tried in African service, but obnoxious on account of their known republican sympathies. The success of Louis Napoleon guaranteed promotion for his friends, and Baraguay d'Hilliers has since flourished under Imperial favor. At the head of his divisions in Italy, he will, it is likely, find opportunities to distinguish himself.

The following order of the day was addressed by Marshal d'Hilliers from his head quarters at Genoa, a few days previous to the battle of Montebello, gained by one of his columns under General Forey, over the Austrians ; the opening French victory of the campaign.

"Soldiers ! In 1796 and 1800 the French army under the orders of General Bonaparte, obtained in Italy glorious victories over the same enemies whom we are about to combat. Several demi-brigades then acquired the designation of ' Terrible' or ' Invincible,' which each of you, by his courage, firmness, and discipline, will endeavor to give to his standard. Soldiers, have confidence in me, as I have in you. Let us show ourselves worthy of France and of the Emperor ; and let us so act that it shall one day be said of us as was said of our fathers, in expressing all titles of glory—'.He belonged to the army of Italy !"

IX.

NAPOLEON III., Emperor of France, is the son of Louis Bonaparte, younger brother of the first Napoleon, and of Hortense Beauharnais, daughter of the Empress Josephine, and afterward known as the Duchess of St. Leu. On the death of Napoleon's only son, the Duke of Reichstadt, Louis Napoleon became the nearest representative of his great uncle. His mother, the Duchess de St. Leu, cherished the hope of his elevation to her death, and her constant influence was exerted to prepare him for the attainment and preservation of the throne which her imperial step-father lost at Waterloo. As early as the fall of Charles X., Louis Napoleon, in company with his brother, endeavored to excite a revolution in Italy, and the brother fell in that abortive attempt. The ambitious prince devoted his energies, in the prime of manhood, to preparation for what, with Napoleonic fatalism, he deemed his " destiny " in the future. His different literary productions, particularly *Les Rêveries Politiques* and *Des Idées Napoléoniennes*, were obviously written to impress his countrymen with the conviction that he not only comprehended, but was disposed to follow the example of his great predecessor, in his measures for the aggrandizement of France. " I would have," said he, in the *Rêveries*, "a government which should embrace all the advantages of a republic without entailing its inconveniences ; a government that should be strong without despotism, free without anarchy, independent without conquests—the people enjoying real and organized sovereignty, as the electoral source, guardian, and regulator of all power ; two chambers, composing a Legislature, the first elected, but certain conditions necessary to the other, founded on services rendered, or experience gained by its eligible members." With such weaponry of assurances, Louis Napoleon opperated from his mother's little court in her Swiss chateau, until, in the year 1836, he had succeeded in enlisting wide-spread sympathy and organizing a secret combination of Bonapartists and republicans, ramified throughout many districts of France, and embracing soldiers in most of the regiments. At what he conceived a favorable moment, his first revolutionary attempt was made by a sudden rising in Strasbourg, near the Swiss border in France, which might have succeeded had it not been for Louis Napoleon's own imprudence. Entering the fortress, on the evening of October 28, 1836, he was secreted by his adherents, and, on the 30th, presented himself suddenly before the barracks in presence of the Fourth Regiment of Artillerists. He was dressed in the well-known military costume of Napoleon I., and, boldly advancing, cried out, " Soldiers a great revolution is commencing at this moment. The nephew of the Emperor is before you ! He comes to put himself at your head. He has arrived on the soil of France to restore to it liberty and glory. The time has come when you must act or die for a great cause—the cause of the people. Soldiers of the Fourth Artillery, can the nephew of the Emperor count upon you ? "

The capital subscribed for amounts to 2,367,000,000 francs : For Paris, 1,547,000,000f. ; for the departments, about 700,000,000f. For 10f. of rente, 80,000,000f.; for larger sums, 2,227,000,000.

As an average of war expenses on the part of a single nation, we may quote the financial results of English belligerency during 127 years, terminating with the battle of Waterloo, 65 years of which time were spent in actual hostilities.

The war of 1688, ended by the Treaty of Ryswick, lasted nine years, and cost....	£36,000,000
War of the Spanish Succession, from 1702 to 1713, cost........	62,500,000
Spanish War of 1782, settled at Aix-la-Chapelle, cost......	55,000,000
Seven Years' War, 1756 to 1763, settled by treaty of Paris, cost.........'.......	112,000,000
American Colonial War, 1775 to 1783, cost	186,000,000
War against the French Republic, 1793 to 1802, cost...........................	469,000,000
War against Napoleon Bonaparte, 1803 to 1815............................	1,159,000,000
Total..	£2,023,500,000

To support this term of sixty-five years fighting, the British government borrowed £834,000,000, and taxed its subjects during the same period, £21,189,000,000. Such statistics present an approximate idea of the cost and consequences of war among civilized nations.

ANNOUNCEMENT TO THE PUBLIC.

Arrangements have been made for reliable information connected with European affairs; and in the event of a continuance of the Present War, or its advance into Central Europe, we shall issue, from time to time, in pamphlet form, such matter of Important Interest as may be necessary to a

COMPLETE HISTORICAL UNDERSTANDING
OF
EUROPEAN RELATIONS.

EMBRACING

REVIEWS OF THE VARIOUS STRUGGLES FOR LIBERTY AND NATIONALITY

in different countries of the Old World.

IN PREPARATION,

A LIFE OF JOSEPH GARIBALDI.
THE ITALIAN PATRIOT.

Containing his Adventures and Services in Two Worlds.

The pamphlets that we shall issue on this subject, will be embellished with PORTRAITS, and other engravings of interesting scenes and objects, and will contain carefully prepared Maps and Diagrams.

CPSIA information can be obtained
at www.ICGtesting.com
Printed in the USA
BVHW070419020119
536776BV00013B/1799/P